A COOKBOOK

A COOKBOOK

BOLD, UNSERIOUS, DELICIOUS FOOD FOR EVERY OCCASION.

HODDER &
STOUGHTON

CONTENTS

Tom Jackson (left) and Harry Bamber (right), the co-heads of Twisted, met for the very first time at the front door of Harry's old flat in London, England, on a crisp January day in 2016. From there, Tom, a talented cook from Birmingham, and Harry, a passionate videographer, set about making some food videos and publishing their endeavours on social media. In just six weeks they gained one million followers.

Today, Twisted is a team of twelve based in east London, and their following has grown to over 30 million people worldwide. From Cairo to Mexico City, from Sydney to São Paulo, all are drawn to Twisted's refreshing, fun approach to cooking and eating.

INTRODUCTION

"To hell with fashion, trends and gastronomic one-upmanship! Cooking, as well as eating, should be fun."

KEITH FLOYD

Ever scrambled the eggs in your carbonara in a hungover stupor and tried washing the spaghetti under the tap? Ever grilled a lasagne for an hour instead of roasting it? Ever put beef in the trifle? We've all been there… haven't we? Well, we're here to take the pressure off, to reassure, and hopefully put a smile on your face.

The world can be a serious place and the food world especially so – brimming with ego, puffed-out bravado, moth-eaten rules and, as Keith says, 'gastronomic one-upmanship'. At Twisted, we're not too fussed with all that. For us, *the good life* does not result from this season's fad diet – counting calories with an abacus – or slaving over the latest (probably quite expensive) 'wellness' ethos. We are passionate about reminding people that it's all right to indulge from time to time and, most importantly, to *have fun*. Cooking and eating the food that you love makes you happy, and it's so important to do what you love in life.

We are living in an era of hyper self-consciousness; a time when the things we say, the way we look, in fact everything we do, are scrutinised by the entire world. Now and then, if only occasionally, we need to be reminded that it's okay to have a good time. Remember that old maxim 'everything in moderation'? It still stands. If you are going to have a day off, or treat yourself, you may as well do it properly.

Sometimes, if we're a bit knackered after work, we want to rattle through dinner as quickly as humanly possible. Other times? We want to really labour over it, throw the kitchen sink at it, perhaps alongside a good bottle of wine and some nibbles. Either way, cooking is a ritualistic, rollercoaster love–hate relationship that we would literally die without. So wouldn't it be great if you could throw out the rulebook, do whatever you wanted, and fall in love with it all over again?

Putting a twist on something is nothing new. Just look to the origins of some of our 'national' dishes – conceptually, fusion food has been around for centuries. Banh Mi, the iconic and world-famous Vietnamese sandwich, depends on a crusty French baguette and a swipe of pâté as a foil for its grilled meat, herbs and pickles. The vindaloo – a dish adopted and beloved by a handful of nations along the spice trade route – derives from an old Portuguese dish: *carne de vinha d'alhos*. Who do these dishes *really* belong to? Fish and chips – the Brits claim it, but it is rumoured to be a Jewish creation. French fries? First spotted in Belgium. Cheesecake is purportedly Greek, and they say pasta dough was developed in China. Go figure!

Retracing the steps of our collective food lineage is a lesson in how, over time, our culinary stories have slowly become intertwined. In today's hyperconnected world, though, our ability to learn from one another, and to borrow food knowledge, is far greater; this process is much quicker, easier and more justified than ever. That is a really exciting prospect for cooks.

The more we share, the more the spotlight centres on the preservation of distinct, separate food cultures. It's important, for sure, but to obsess over it means that food remains landlocked or fixed in time – that it can't evolve, change or, as a result, improve. Amid all the fake news, we all crave unearthing traditional, 'real' food that encapsulates history and meaning; food that transports us to a specific time and place. We love a dusty, first-edition Mughal cookbook as much as the next culinary crusader, but the truth is that the world today is also hungry for something new. Culture isn't static, so food – its cornerstone – shouldn't be either. Inauthenticity in food is often dismissed out-of-hand, but in it there is much to be celebrated: it represents innovation, experimentation and, ultimately, progression.

Nowhere is this conversation more energetic than on social media. Today's digital foodscape has broadened our horizons, exposing us to new cuisines, cultures and, most importantly, the people behind them, as they broadcast their views to the world. The overwhelming diversity of these opinions reminds us of the subjectivity of food. There really is no right or wrong way to cook, provided it's right for you. In this, there is a stark reminder of quite how different we all are, but that concurrently, through food, we are all one and the same.

In our cookbook, we are four people writing recipes and stories, three illustrators, three photographers, three stylists, twelve staff and over 30 million people all over the world. It is both a distillation and a reflection of these converging and contrasting points of view. So, if it ever feels a bit wild, that's the point. This is precisely what today's debate looks like.

THE RECIPES

Twisted is about much more than putting a splash of fish sauce in your bolognese (although you crack on!) or some balsamic vinegar on your strawberries (posh!). For us, it really is just an attitude to cooking (and living) that makes it considerably more enjoyable. It's about questioning everything. Why do I have to put that in now? Why can't I cook this on top of loads of onions? What's wrong with making a massive one? Sometimes it can feel like you're shackled by the way something looks in the photo, or the way someone says you have to do it, but as we've established, you make your own rules!

Whether it's making your pasta salad look like a massive flying bruschetta (p.180), baking some Camembert directly on top of your spaghetti (p.173), or making a pakora look a bit like a crab (p.34), there are ways in which you can reinvigorate your cooking that are not as reductive as merely swapping one ingredient out for another. It could well be an unconventional way of cooking something, or serving it so that it looks like something else. In short, we fiercely encourage you to play with your food.

Some of the recipes are more ambitious than others, requiring a little more attention, a little more time, or a few new ingredients; and some are dead simple, that you can whip up in a flash (or when you're really hungover). The approach, though, is the same: we are always trying something a little different. We think it's important to broaden your horizons with new ingredients, so get yourself down to a good Asian supermarket, if you can, and buy that Chinkiang vinegar. You won't regret it. Everyone cooks differently, so we haven't given you the 'difficulty level' of any recipes. Anyone can make the recipes in this book. So give it a read and give them a try!

It's important to clarify that, although we offer precise measurements and instructions, we strongly encourage you to alter any recipes in order to suit your tastes; changing ingredients or quantities to satisfy your whims. The irony isn't lost on us – we don't really follow recipes, so why should you? We have tested ours to the hilt, so if you follow them to the letter, we can assure you that you won't be disappointed (but we won't be offended if you don't – quite the opposite!). Twisted is not about being exclusive, preachy or prescriptive. We want to inspire you to be creative and to do it your way, not tell you what to do. That wouldn't be any fun.

THE CHAPTERS

We have divided our book into three clear, easily digestible sections:

BASICS (p.16) is the place to turn for some of our essentials: milk buns, a classic 'forget-about-it' oven-cooked ragu, a delicious ketchup, the best fried chicken burger sauce you've never had, etc. These recipes either feature several times throughout the book, or are just really nice accompaniments to our food and don't fit anywhere else! Not your average set of 'kitchen staples' – but if that's what you're looking for, Delia has got you covered.

We firmly believe that food tastes best when shared with loved ones. As such, we've devoted the first half of our book to the social aspect of food: ***OCCASIONS*** (p.30). Whether you've got your vegan pal coming over for Meat-Free Monday, you're trying to impress your mates down the park at your Picnic or it's Game Day this weekend and 'you got nothin' – we've got your back!

But what happens when the party's over? ***INGREDIENTS*** (p.160). Sometimes, when you don't fancy pushing the boat out and trying something completely out there, you tend to fall back on the things you love the most. That's all right. In fact, we understand to such an extent, we've devoted half the book to it. Chicken, Chocolate, Wraps, Fruit, Potatoes and Pasta: these are easy recipes using the world's favourite ingredients.

OK, that's it. Have fun!

Tag us in your creations! #twistedcookbook

 @Twisted

 @JungleTwisted

BAS

ics

BREAD

POTATO ROLLS p.35

MAKES 7 BURGER-SIZED ROLLS

450g (1lb) potatoes, peeled and diced into 3cm (1in) chunks

30g (2 tbsp) unsalted butter, plus extra for greasing

325g (2⅓ cups) strong bread flour, plus extra for dusting

2½ tbsp caster (superfine) sugar

1 sachet (7g) fast-action dried yeast

1 tsp fine sea salt

¼ tsp ground turmeric

1 large egg

sesame seeds, for sprinkling (optional)

Egg wash:

1 egg, beaten

2 tsp milk

1. Put the potatoes into a medium saucepan with enough cold water to cover. Bring to the boil over a high heat and cook for about 15 minutes, or until the potatoes are tender to the point of a knife. Drain, reserving 5 tbsp of the cooking water, and return to the pan to steam dry.

2. Put the potatoes through a ricer or food mill or mash well with a potato masher. Measure out 250g (1 firmly packed cup) of the mash (this quantity of potatoes should yield about the right amount) and stir in the butter until melted.

3. In a stand mixer, combine the flour, sugar, yeast, salt and turmeric. Add the warm mash to the flour mixture and mix with your hands until combined (some large lumps are OK). Add the egg and the reserved potato cooking water and mix with a dough hook on low speed for about 5 minutes until the dough is soft and slightly sticky.

4. Remove the dough to a floured surface and gently knead until smooth, then shape into a ball and place in a lightly greased bowl. Cover tightly with

clingfilm (plastic wrap) and allow to rise at room temperature until almost doubled in volume, 30–40 minutes.

5. Turn out the dough onto the work surface, dusting with flour only if the dough is too sticky to handle, and divide into 7 equal pieces. Cover with clingfilm and leave to rest for about 15 minutes.

6. Working with 1 piece of dough at a time and keeping the remaining pieces covered, form into smooth, taut rounds. Cover the rounds with clingfilm and leave to rest for another 15 minutes.

7. Line 2 baking trays with baking paper. On a lightly floured surface, firmly press each round into a 9cm (3½in) disc of even thickness, expelling any large pockets of air. Arrange on the prepared baking trays, cover loosely with clingfilm and let rise at room temperature until almost doubled in size, 30–40 minutes.

8. Meanwhile, adjust the oven racks to middle and upper-middle positions and preheat the oven to 220°C/425°F/gas 7.

9. Beat the egg and milk together for the egg wash and brush the rolls with the mixture. Sprinkle with the sesame seeds (if using). Bake for 15–18 minutes until deep golden brown, rotating and switching the baking trays halfway through. Let cool on the trays for 5 minutes, then transfer the rolls to wire racks to cool completely. Best served sliced in half and toasted for a burger.

SLOW-RISE PIZZA DOUGH

MAKES 3 LARGE PIZZA BASES

625g (4½ cups) strong bread flour

2 tbsp caster (superfine) sugar

2 tsp fine sea salt

1 sachet (7g) fast-action dried yeast

420ml (1¾ cups) water

55g (3½ tbsp) unsalted butter

plain (all-purpose) flour, for dusting

1. Combine the flour, sugar, salt and yeast in the bowl of a food processor and pulse until mixed together. Add the water and process for at least 15 seconds until the mixture forms a ball that rides around the bowl. Add the butter and process for another 15–30 seconds until combined.

2. Transfer the dough to a lightly floured work surface and knead until smooth.

3. Divide the dough into 3 equal parts and place each in a freezer bag. Place in the refrigerator and allow to rise for at least 24 hours and up to 5 days.

4. Remove from the refrigerator, shape into balls, and allow to rest at room temperature for at least 2 hours before baking.

5. At least 1 hour before baking, preheat the oven to 220°C/425°F/gas 7 and place a pizza stone, a large flat cast-iron pan or heavy baking sheet in the oven to heat up.

6. On a lightly floured surface, gently press out the dough into a 20cm (8in) circle, leaving a 3cm (1in) rim for the crust.

7. Spread with tomato sauce and toppings of choice, leaving the crust area empty. Slide the pizza onto the hot stone/pan/sheet and bake for 12–15 minutes.

ROSEMARY & GARLIC FOCACCIA

SERVES 6–8

p.67

500g (3½ cups) strong bread flour

350ml (1½ cups) water

3½ tbsp olive oil, plus extra for greasing and drizzling

2 tsp flaked sea salt, plus extra for sprinkling

2 scant tsp fast-action dried yeast

1¼ tsp sugar

4 garlic cloves, thinly sliced

4–5 rosemary sprigs, leaves only

1. In a stand mixer fitted with a hook attachment set on medium speed, mix together the flour, water, oil, salt, yeast and sugar until well combined. Turn the speed to high and knead until the dough comes away from the sides of the bowl.

2. Add the sliced garlic and mix on low speed for 1 minute to combine.

3. Transfer the dough to an oiled bowl and cover with clingfilm (plastic wrap). Let rise for 2 hours, being sure to fold the edges of the dough into the middle every 30 minutes.

4. Grease and line a heavy, deep-sided 33 x 23cm (13 x 9in) baking dish with baking paper and drizzle with more olive oil.

5. When the dough has doubled in size, transfer it to the prepared dish and gently push it out to the edges. If it sprigs back, don't worry – as it rests it will gradually spread out and fill the dish. Cover with clingfilm and set aside to let it double in size again, about 45 minutes–1 hour.

6. Preheat the oven to 200°C/400°F/gas 6.

7. Firmly poke your fingers into the dough all over to create deep indents. Place a little rosemary in each indent and drizzle with more olive oil and sprinkle with sea salt.

8. Bake for 18–20 minutes until golden brown.

9. Let cool in the dish completely before serving.

BREAD

MILK BUNS p.106

MAKES 12 BURGER BUNS OR 24 SLIDERS

240ml (1 cup) whole (full-fat) milk, lukewarm

2 tsp fast-action dried yeast

1 tbsp sugar

3 large eggs: 2 whisked; 1 whisked separately with 1 tsp water for brushing

500g (2 cups) strong bread flour

1½ tsp fine sea salt

85g (generous ⅓ cup) unsalted butter, softened, plus extra for greasing

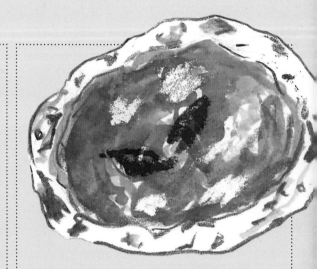

1. Combine the milk, yeast and sugar in a large bowl and mix well. Let sit until slightly frothy, about 5–10 minutes. Add the 2 whisked eggs and stir until combined.

2. Add the flour and salt and mix until well combined, then remove from the bowl and knead to a sticky but soft dough.

3. Knead the softened butter into the dough for about 10–15 minutes until the dough is soft and forms a ball. The dough will absorb all the butter as you knead.

4. Place in a lightly greased bowl and cover with clingfilm (plastic wrap) and let rise in a warm place until doubled in size, about 1 hour.

5. Knock back the dough and divide into 40g (1½oz) balls for sliders, or 80g (3oz) balls for regular burger buns. Flatten each dough ball into a disc, then bring the sides into the middle and roll to seal tight.

6. Preheat the oven to 200°C/400°F/gas 6. Line a baking tray with baking paper.

7. Arrange the dough balls on the prepared tray, spacing them about 3cm (1in) apart. Cover with clingfilm and set aside once again to double in size, about 30–40 minutes.

8. When they have doubled in size, brush the buns gently with the egg wash.

9. Bake for 12–15 minutes until golden brown. Remove from the oven and transfer to a wire rack to cool.

10. Any buns not used immediately will keep well for up to 4 days in an airtight container.

PICKLES

PICKLED JALAPEÑOS

MAKES 1 X 500ML (1 PINT) JAR

250ml (generous 1 cup) malt vinegar

150ml (⅔ cup) water

4 tbsp sugar

1 tbsp fine sea salt

2 fat garlic cloves, sliced

225g (8oz) jalapeños, sliced

1. Put the vinegar, water, sugar, salt and garlic into a small saucepan and bring to the boil, stirring until the sugar has dissolved.

2. Add the jalapeño slices and continue to boil for 2 minutes. Remove from the heat to cool, then pour into a sterilised glass jar.

3. Chill overnight. These keep well in the refrigerator for a couple of weeks.

QUICK PICKLED ONIONS p.207

MAKES 1 x 1L (1¾ PINT) JAR

5 large red onions

300ml (1¼ cups) cider vinegar

300ml (1¼ cups) water

juice of 2 limes

4 tbsp caster (superfine) sugar

1 tbsp flaked sea salt

8 black peppercorns

1 tsp yellow mustard seeds

1. Peel, halve and thinly slice the red onions and set aside.

2. Put the remaining ingredients into a medium saucepan and bring to a simmer, stirring to dissolve the sugar and salt.

3. Pack the onions into a sterilised 1l (1¾ pint) jar and pour the hot pickling liquid over, ensuring all the onions are submerged. Let cool, then seal tightly and refrigerate for at least 2 hours.

4. These are best after 1–2 days, and keep well for a couple of weeks in the refrigerator.

PICKLES

BREAD & BUTTER PICKLES

MAKES 1 X 500ML (1 PINT) JAR

 p.203

500g (1lb 2 oz) ridged cucumbers, trimmed at both ends

1½ tbsp fine sea salt

½ white onion, sliced

200ml (generous ¾ cup) water

200ml (generous ¾ cup) cider vinegar

150g (¾ cup) caster (superfine) sugar

a pinch of ground turmeric

½ tsp celery seeds

1 heaped tsp yellow mustard seeds

8 black peppercorns

1. Grab yourself a fluted cutter or mandoline and slice the cucumbers 4mm (⅛in) thick.

2. Place the cucumber slices in a bowl and toss gently with the salt and sliced onion, then transfer to a large sieve set over a bowl to drain for at least 1 hour.

3. Transfer the salted veg to a large bowl and run through a few changes of water, then drain and place into a sterilised jar.

4. Put the remaining ingredients into a small saucepan and bring to a simmer. Remove from the heat, then carefully pour the hot brine into the jar, completely submerging the cucumbers and onions. Let cool completely at room temperature, then seal tightly and refrigerate overnight.

5. These keep well for a couple of weeks.

DILL PICKLES

MAKES 1 X 500ML (1 PINT) JAR

500g (1lb 2 oz) ridged cucumbers, trimmed at both ends

1½ tbsp fine sea salt

4 garlic cloves, roughly chopped

a handful of fresh dill stalks

200ml (generous ¾ cup) distilled white vinegar

200ml (generous ¾ cup) water

2–3 tbsp caster (superfine) sugar

½ tsp celery seeds

1 heaped tsp yellow mustard seeds

1 bay leaf

1. Grab yourself a fluted cutter or mandoline and slice the cucumbers 4mm (⅛in) thick.

2. Place the cucumber slices in a bowl and toss gently with the salt, then transfer to a large sieve set over a bowl to drain for at least 1 hour.

3. Transfer the salted cucumbers to a large bowl and run through a few changes of water, then drain and place into a sterilised jar along with the garlic and dill.

4. Put the remaining ingredients into a small saucepan and bring to a simmer. Remove from the heat, then carefully pour the hot brine into the jar, completely submerging the cucumbers. Let cool completely at room temperature, then seal tightly and refrigerate overnight.

5. These keep well for a couple of weeks.

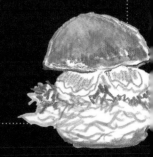

SAUCES

MEAT RAGU

MAKES 1KG (6 CUPS)

500g (1lb 2 oz) minced (ground) beef

500g (1lb 2 oz) minced (ground) pork

3 tbsp olive oil

1 large onion, very finely chopped

1 large carrot, very finely diced

2 celery sticks, very finely diced

200g (7oz) pancetta or streaky bacon, cut into very small pieces

3 garlic cloves, crushed

350ml (1½ cups) red wine

4 tbsp tomato purée (paste)

1 x 400g (14oz) can chopped tomatoes

300ml (1¼ cups) rich beef stock

1½ tsp demerara (turbinado) sugar

salt and freshly ground black pepper, to taste

1. Preheat the oven to 140°C/275°F/gas 1.

2. Mix together the beef and pork until well combined.

3. Heat 2 tbsp olive oil in a large frying pan (skillet) over a medium heat. Take small chunks of the meat mixture and fry them like meatballs, just to get some colour on each side. Do this in 2 batches so as not to overcrowd the pan, keeping the cooked chunks in a bowl to the side. When you've browned all the meat add it all back to the pan, breaking up the chunks with a wooden spoon and cooking it through, about 5 minutes. Transfer all the meat to a large bowl and set aside.

4. Add the remaining 1 tbsp oil to the pan, then add the onion, carrot and celery with a pinch of salt and fry until soft and sweet, about 20–30 minutes, then remove from the pan and add to the bowl with the meat.

5. Heat a large casserole dish (with a lid) over a medium-high heat. Add the pancetta and fry until the fat has rendered and it is starting to crisp, about 5 minutes, then add the garlic and fry for 30 seconds until fragrant. Return the reserved meat and veg to the pan, drawing the garlic through the mixture to stop it from catching. When everything is hot, pour in the wine and let it evaporate almost completely, then stir in the tomato purée and cook for 2–3 minutes, until the raw aroma has gone. Add the tomatoes, beef stock, sugar and another pinch of salt and bring to a simmer.

6. Place the lid on the casserole, leaving it slightly ajar, and transfer to the oven to cook for at least 4 hours, until the sauce is thick, unctuous and rich. Season to taste towards the end of cooking.

GARLIC & HERB MAYO p.203

MAKES 300G (GENEROUS 1¼ CUPS)

300g (generous 1¼ cups) mayonnaise

2 tbsp finely chopped chives

1½ tbsp finely chopped tarragon

1 tsp sugar

½ tsp black pepper

½ garlic clove, crushed to a paste with a little salt

1 tsp lemon juice

1. Thoroughly combine everything in a bowl, then cover with clingfilm (plastic wrap) and leave to sit for 30 minutes at room temperature. Stir again, then use.

2. Best eaten fresh, but keeps well for 2–3 days in the refrigerator.

SAUCES

EVERYTHING GARLICKY TOMATO SAUCE p.49

MAKES 1L (GENEROUS 4 CUPS)

125ml (½ cup) olive oil

6 fat garlic cloves, green sprouts removed, thinly sliced

4 x 400g (14oz) cans good-quality plum tomatoes

1½ tsp sugar

salt, to taste

1. Put the cold olive oil and sliced garlic into a large heavy saucepan and set over a low heat. After about 6–8 minutes, the garlic should be very lightly sizzling, translucent and sticky and should have taken on a slightly darker colour, but should not be brown.

2. Chuck in the tomatoes, sugar and a good pinch of salt and slowly cook for 2 hours, or more if you have time, stirring occasionally and topping up with water if it's looking at all dry. The final sauce should be well reduced and thick with a pleasing film of oil on top.

3. Blend your sauce with a hand-held stick (immersion) blender until smooth and transfer to sterilised jars. Unopened, it will keep for up to 1 year; once opened, it will keep for 3–4 days in the refrigerator.

FRIED CHICKEN BURGER SAUCE

MAKES 200G (SCANT 1 CUP)

100g (scant ½ cup) tomato ketchup

100g (scant ½ cup) mayonnaise

½–1 tsp Mr Naga Hot Pepper Pickle, to taste

1. Combine the ingredients in a bowl.

2. Eat with fried chicken.

STICK BLENDER MAYO

MAKES 300ML (1¼ CUPS)

2 large egg yolks (as fresh as you can get)

1 tbsp English mustard

1 tsp white wine vinegar

1 tsp lemon juice

200ml (generous ¾ cup) neutral oil

3½ tbsp olive oil

salt, to taste

1. To a large, narrow, shatterproof jug (Pyrex measuring jugs are good), add the egg yolks, mustard, vinegar, lemon juice and a pinch of salt in that order. Gently pour the oils on top, trying not to disturb the ingredients at the bottom.

2. Insert a hand-held stick (immersion) blender right to the bottom and turn it on. Hold on tight! Leave it at the bottom for roughly 5 seconds then gradually bring it up to the top, incorporating the oils as you go. At this stage it'll look like a few big blobs of mayonnaise surrounded by a small amount of oil. Be careful – don't over-blend or it'll split. Sad times. Turn off the blender.

3. Scoop the mixture into a bowl and finish by stirring well with a spoon. Splash in a little water or lemon juice if it's looking a little stiff.

4. Alternatively, use a food processor for the whole process. Simply place everything (apart from the oils) in the bowl and slowly drizzle in the oils (starting with the neutral oil) with the motor running until you have a thick, smooth emulsion.

5. Check for seasoning and adjust if necessary. Best eaten straight away, but keeps well for up to a week.

SAUCES

4-INGREDIENT NACHO SAUCE

MAKES 500ML (GENEROUS 2 CUPS)

1 x 400g (14oz) can evaporated milk

250g (2½ cups) Double Gloucester or Cheddar cheese, grated

1½ tbsp cornflour (cornstarch)

2 tbsp hot sauce or 30g (¼ cup) chopped jalapeños

1. Empty the evaporated milk into a saucepan and set over a medium heat.

2. Meanwhile, toss the cheese with the cornflour until well coated.

3. Add the cheese to the hot milk and stir continuously until thickened, then remove from the heat and stir in the hot sauce or jalapeños.

4. Immediately pour all over your nachos.

BÉCHAMEL SAUCE

MAKES ABOUT 500ML (GENEROUS 2 CUPS)

600ml (2½ cups) whole (full-fat) milk

½ medium onion

4 cloves (optional)

6 peppercorns

1 bay leaf, scrunched up a bit to release the oils

50g (3½ tbsp) unsalted butter

40g (4½ tbsp) plain (all-purpose) flour

salt and freshly ground black pepper, to taste

1. Pour the milk into a saucepan and add the onion (studded with the cloves, if using), peppercorns and bay leaf. Bring just to a simmer, then remove from the heat, cover and let steep for around 1 hour. Strain the milk into a jug through a fine sieve and keep warm.

2. Heat the butter in a saucepan until foaming, then beat in the flour with a wooden spoon to form a paste, or roux. Cook for 30 seconds or so, until it smells biscuity.

3. Add a large splash of the infused milk and beat until very smooth. Keep adding the milk, a good splash at a time, beating out any lumps before adding more.

4. When all the milk has been incorporated, season with salt and pepper, to taste. Keep cooking over a low heat for around 10 minutes, stirring frequently.

5. At this point, let your imagination run wild. Feel free to add cheese, herbs, nutmeg, or whatever.

TWISTED KETCHUP p.228

MAKES 1.25L (5 CUPS)

3 x 400g (14oz) cans plum tomatoes

250g (9oz) apples, peeled, cored and chopped

1 large fennel bulb (about 250g/9oz), coarsely chopped

250g (9oz) onions, coarsely chopped

1 tbsp hot smoked paprika

1 tbsp freshly ground black pepper

1 tbsp flaked sea salt

225ml (scant 1 cup) malt vinegar

250g (1¼ cups) granulated sugar

1. Put all the ingredients into a stainless steel stockpot and bring to a simmer. Reduce the heat and cook for about 2 hours, topping up with a little water from time to time if necessary.

2. Let cool, then blitz in a food processor or with a hand-held stick (immersion) blender until smooth. Pass through a sieve and transfer to sterilised jars/bottles.

3. Keeps well for 2–3 weeks in the refrigerator.

SAUCES

TROPICAL HOT SAUCE

MAKES 500ML (GENEROUS 2 CUPS)

6 fat garlic cloves, unpeeled

150g (5½oz) white onion, roughly chopped

200g (7oz) pineapple flesh, roughly chopped

10–12 Scotch bonnet chillies, deseeded (with a few left unseeded for the brave)

300ml (1¼ cups) distilled white vinegar (cider vinegar and rice wine vinegar are also good)

200ml (generous ¾ cup) water

2 passion fruit

100g (3½oz) mango flesh

salt, to taste

1. Roast the garlic cloves in a dry pan until the skins have charred a little in places. Watch the garlic flesh doesn't burn – it will ruin the flavour of your hot sauce. Cool, then peel and set aside.

2. Place the onion, pineapple and half of the chillies in a small saucepan. Set aside 3½ tbsp of the vinegar and add the rest to the saucepan along with the water and a very good pinch of salt. Bring to the boil and cook over a lively heat for 10 minutes. The liquid should have reduced byabout half. Remove from the heat to cool completely.

3. Halve and scoop out the seeds and pulp from the passion fruit and pass through a sieve. Place the pulp in a blender, along with the mango, the cooled pineapple/chilli mixture (including the reduced liquid), the remaining chillies, peeled garlic cloves and the reserved vinegar. Process to a very smooth purée – it should be the texture of a thin smoothie. Taste for seasoning and adjust if necessary – it may need a little more vinegar or salt. It should taste very tropical, hot, zippy and full-flavoured.

4. Transfer to a sterilised bottle and refrigerate for up to 3 months.

RANCH TWO WAYS

MAKES ABOUT 400G (1¾ CUPS)

Dirty Ranch:

100g (scant ½ cup) Greek-style yoghurt

300g (generous 1¼ cups) mayonnaise

½ tsp garlic powder

½ tsp black pepper

1 tbsp lemon juice

1 tbsp Italian seasoning (Italian-style herb blend)

¼ tsp cayenne pepper

salt, to taste

Posh Ranch:

200g (scant 1 cup) sour cream

200g (scant 1 cup) mayonnaise

1 garlic clove crushed

½ tsp black pepper

1½ tsp white wine vinegar

1 tbsp finely chopped fresh dill

1 tbsp finely chopped flat-leaf parsley

1 tbsp finely chopped tarragon

1 tbsp finely chopped chive

salt, to taste

1. For both recipes, simply whisk everything together and season to taste. Job done.

2. These are best eaten fresh, but keep well for 2–3 days in the refrigerator.

OTHER BITS

GARLIC PARSLEY BUTTER

MAKES 125G (GENEROUS ½ CUP)

125g (generous ½ cup) unsalted butter, softened

2 fat garlic cloves, very finely chopped or grated

3 tbsp finely chopped flat-leaf parsley

½ tsp fine sea salt

1. Place the butter, garlic, parsley and salt in a bowl and thoroughly beat with an electric whisk or a wooden spoon to combine.

2. Tip the mixture onto a square of baking paper or clingfilm (plastic wrap), roll it around the butter to form a sausage shape, then twist the ends to seal.

3. Store for up to 3 days in the refrigerator or up to 1 month in the freezer.

BBQ RUB

MAKES 275G (1½ CUPS)

1½ tsp black peppercorns

1 tsp coriander seeds

1 tsp cumin seeds

1 tbsp fennel seeds

150g (¾ cup) soft light brown sugar

100g (generous ⅓ cup) fine sea salt

½ tsp garlic powder

1 tsp mustard powder

1½ tsp cayenne pepper

1 heaped tbsp smoked paprika

1 tsp dried oregano

1. In a heavy dry pan, toast the peppercorns, coriander, cumin and fennel seeds until they smell amazing – there should be an almost incense-like aroma coming from them and the cumin seeds should be crackling.

2. In a mortar and pestle (or spice grinder), finely bash up all the toasted spices to a coarse powder. Transfer them to a bowl, add all the other ingredients and mix thoroughly.

3. Keeps well in an airtight jar for 2–3 months.

CHEAT'S BUTTERMILK BRINE

MAKES 1L (GENEROUS 4 CUPS)

50g (¼ cup) fine sea salt

3 tbsp caster (superfine) sugar

1 tsp black peppercorns

1 fresh bay leaf

1 tsp fennel seeds

100ml (generous ⅓ cup) water

6 tbsp lemon juice

900ml (scant 4 cups) whole (full-fat) milk

½ medium onion, sliced

1. Put the salt, sugar, peppercorns, bay leaf and fennel seeds into a small saucepan along with the water and bring to a simmer. Remove from the heat and let cool completely, then briefly chill in the refrigerator until cold.

2. Combine the cold mixture with the remaining ingredients and let sit for 30 minutes at room temperature.

3. Use immediately as required or refrigerate for up to 1 week in an airtight container.

Occa

Meat-Free Monday

Super Veggies

Europeans may have been dabbling in plant-based cookery for some time, but for the spiritual home of herbivorous dining, one has to look to Asia. Though there are hundreds of distinct leaf-leaning heritages, the kings of vegetarianism are surely the Jain monks of India, who raise the practice of not harming creatures to giddy new heights. Instead of squashing insects, Jains sweep them out of their way with brooms, proving that - to a super veggie - every animal is just as important as the next.

SPICY CAULIFLOWER PAKORA BURGERS

Haweli is an Indian restaurant on the Hagley Road in Birmingham, England, owned by a geneticist who often helps out behind the bar. They make excellent pakoras, amongst other things. This is our version. Tossing all the vegetables in the flours first and using cold sparkling water (as per Japanese tempura batter) keeps these crisp and light.

SERVES 6

250g (9oz) cauliflower, broken into florets and thinly sliced

2 large red onions, thinly sliced from root to tip

a large handful of fresh coriander (cilantro), roughly chopped

a small handful of fresh curry leaves

2 green chillies, finely chopped

350g (2¾ cups) chickpea (gram) flour

1 tsp baking powder

1½ tbsp flaked sea salt

1½ tbsp coriander seeds, bashed a bit but mostly left whole

1½ tbsp whole cumin seeds

1½ tbsp ground cumin

2 tsp Kashmiri (mild) chilli powder

1 tsp garam masala

½ tsp ajwain seeds, ground

½ tsp ground turmeric

about 350ml (1½ cups) cold, sparkling water

neutral oil, for deep-frying

To serve:
Potato Rolls (p.20)
shredded lettuce
sliced tomatoes
sliced cucumber
Roasted Cumin Raita (p.120)
mango chutney

1. Place the sliced cauliflower in a large heatproof bowl and cover with boiling water. Leave to steep for 10 minutes or so, then drain well and pat the slices very dry with kitchen paper.

2. Place the onions, par-cooked cauliflower, fresh coriander, curry leaves and green chilli in a large, wide bowl.

3. In a separate, smaller bowl, combine the chickpea flour, baking powder, salt and all of the spices. Tip this mixture into the vegetables and toss everything in the spiced flour until evenly covered.

4. Gradually add the sparkling water and mix until there are no more pockets of flour and the batter coats everything evenly. The mixture should be slightly loose, so adjust with more water if necessary.

5. Heat enough oil for deep-frying in a deep, heavy saucepan to 175°C (350°F). Grab a fistful of the battered mixture and very carefully release into the oil, rubbing the mix lightly between your fingers as you do so in order to create a large surface area. Fry your creation for 6–8 minutes, turning from time to time, until golden brown and crisp. Remove with a slotted spoon to briefly drain on kitchen paper, then transfer to a wire rack. Repeat with the remaining mixture until you have 6 pakoras – they should be massive and gnarly, dwarfing the buns they're destined for.

6. Load into the potato rolls with the remaining garnishes and demolish!

RED PEPPER VS SPINACH & RICOTTA LASAGNE

Vegetarian lasagnes are quicker to make than the meat-laced versions and just as satisfying. We loved the prospect of both of these fillings so much that we decided to pit them against each other in the same dish – it was delicious. One bright and sweet; the other mellow, earthy and rich.

SERVES 6

butter, for greasing

6–8 fresh lasagne pasta sheets

2 x 125g (4½oz) fresh
mozzarella balls

30g (½ cup) grated Parmesan,
for topping

Sweet red pepper filling:

4 tbsp plus 1 tsp olive oil

2 medium onions, thinly sliced

1 red chilli, deseeded and sliced

3–4 sweet red peppers, thinly sliced

3 garlic cloves, sliced

1kg (2lb 3oz) fresh tomatoes, peeled,
deseeded and roughly chopped

a handful of fresh basil, torn

salt, to taste

White sauce:

70g (scant ⅓ cup) unsalted butter

70g (generous ½ cup) plain
(all-purpose) flour

1l (generous 4 cups) whole (full-fat)
milk

¼ fresh nutmeg, finely grated

salt and freshly ground black
pepper, to taste

Spinach and ricotta filling:

600g (1lb 5oz) spinach

350g (1½ cups) ricotta cheese

100g (1½ cups) Parmesan, grated

¼ fresh nutmeg, finely grated

50g (⅓ cup) pine nuts, toasted

salt and freshly ground black
pepper, to taste

1. First, make the red pepper filling. Heat 4 tbsp of the olive oil in a large saucepan over a medium heat, add the onions along with a pinch of salt and cook for about 10 minutes, stirring frequently, until soft and sweet. Stir through the chilli and red peppers and another pinch of salt and cook, partially covered with a lid, for 25 minutes, or until the peppers have broken down.

2. Push the pepper mixture to the side of the pan and add the garlic along with the remaining 1 tsp olive oil. Fry until just starting to colour, then chuck in the tomatoes and season with a pinch of salt. Stir through the whole mixture to combine, partially cover with a lid and cook for another 20 minutes or so until the tomatoes have broken down into a rich sauce. Stir through the basil and remove from the heat.

3. Next, make your white sauce. Heat the butter in a non-stick saucepan over a medium heat until foaming, then add the flour. Stir together and cook for 1–2 minutes, or until it smells biscuity and the rawness of the flour has gone. Gradually add the milk, whisking away any lumps as you do so. When the milk is fully incorporated, season well with salt and black pepper. Bring to a simmer, then reduce the heat and cook for 10 minutes or so, stirring frequently, until thickened. Grate in the nutmeg, then cover and set aside.

4. For the spinach and ricotta filling, place the spinach in a large saucepan over a medium heat and cook until wilted. Let cool, then squeeze out the excess water and transfer to a food processor. Pulse to chop a bit (you can also do this by hand), then add the remaining ingredients and season to taste. Pulse until smoothish, then add about 150ml (⅔ cup) of the white sauce to loosen. Set aside.

5. Preheat the oven to 190°C/375°F/gas 5.

6. Grease a 23 x 30cm (9 x 12in) lasagne dish with butter, then spoon in a thin layer of white sauce. Cover with a layer of pasta sheets, then add half of the red pepper sauce along with another few tbsp of white sauce. Rip over a third of the mozzarella. Layer more pasta sheets on top then spoon in half of the spinach and ricotta sauce. Repeat. After the second layer of spinach and ricotta is in, top with a final layer of pasta. Spoon the remaining white sauce over the top and cover with Parmesan and any remaining mozzarella.

7. Tightly cover the dish with foil and bake in the oven for 30 minutes, then remove the foil and bake for a further 15 minutes, or until nicely browned on top. Remove from the oven and let rest for 15 minutes (if you can bear the wait), then serve. Enjoy!

MUSHROOM CHEESESTEAKS

p.37

Mushrooms are mysterious things; they are neither plant nor animal, get up to all sorts of weird stuff, and their spores are technically capable of surviving the vacuum of space. This could potentially mean they have floated on solar winds from other worlds, but don't quote us on this. Whether or not they are aliens, they are delicious and make a superb alternative to meat in these guilt-free cheesesteaks.

SERVES 4

20g (¾oz) dried porcini mushrooms

2 tbsp vegetable oil, or more as needed

1 medium onion, thinly sliced

1 green pepper, thinly sliced

300g (10½oz) oyster mushrooms, very thinly sliced

300g (10½oz) shiitake mushrooms, very thinly sliced

300g (10½oz) portobello mushrooms, very thinly sliced

1 tsp garlic powder

50g (3½ tbsp) unsalted butter

1½ tbsp soy sauce

a splash of sherry or Shaoxing rice wine

salt and freshly ground black pepper, to taste

4 bread rolls, toasted and buttered, to serve

Cheese sauce:

300g (2½ cups) provolone or Emmental cheese, grated

1 tsp cornflour (cornstarch)

200ml (generous ¾ cup) evaporated milk

1 tsp vinegary hot sauce (such as Frank's)

1. Soak the porcini in 250ml (generous 1 cup) hot water for 30 minutes, then squeeze out the mushrooms with your hand and fine-strain the soaking liquid into a cup. Set the liquid aside and finely chop the rehydrated porcini.

2. In a large, heavy sauté pan, heat 1 tbsp of the oil over a low-medium heat, add the onion and pepper and fry for about 20 minutes until very soft and golden. Add the chopped porcini and fry for a further 5 minutes. Remove from the pan and set aside in a large bowl.

3. Get the pan back up to a really high heat and add the remaining 1 tbsp of oil. Keeping the mushroom varieties separate, sear them in batches, adding more oil as necessary. Allow them to crisp a little then move them around and cook out some of their moisture. Don't overdo it – you want them to be cooked but still juicy. When everything looks good, stir through the garlic powder and cook briefly then remove from the pan and place in the bowl with the peppers and onions.

4. Pour the porcini soaking water into the pan and reduce by half over a high heat. Add the butter, soy sauce and sherry or rice wine. Stir through the mushrooms, peppers and onions just to warm through, then remove from the heat and season to taste.

5. To make the cheese sauce, toss the cheese with the cornflour and place in a saucepan with the evaporated milk. Stir over a very gentle heat until the cheese has melted and the sauce is gently bubbling. Stir in the hot sauce and remove from the heat.

6. Serve the hot mushroom mixture in toasted buttered rolls, topped with the cheese sauce, and extra hot sauce, if you like.

BBQ AUBERGINE PARMIGIANA

p.41

Sicily is a beguiling island, rich with history and a food culture reflecting millennia of colonisation. The Greeks, Normans and Moors have all passed through; it was the latter who brought the aubergine (eggplant) to the island and the rest of the Mediterranean. Our version of this ancient 'fusion' recipe introduces yet another element – the sweet smoke of American barbecue.

SERVES 4

5 tbsp olive oil

1 large onion, thinly sliced

3 garlic cloves, finely crushed

2 red chillies, thinly sliced

3 x 400g (14oz) cans plum tomatoes (as fancy as you can afford), crushed

250ml (generous 1 cup) barbecue sauce

4 aubergines (eggplants), trimmed and sliced lengthways into 5mm (¼-in) thick slice

2 tbsp BBQ Rub **(p.29)**

2 x 100g (3½oz) balls fresh mozzarella, drained and torn into small chunks

50g (¾ cup) Parmesan, finely grated

salt and freshly ground black pepper, to taste

1. In a saucepan with a lid, heat 2 tbsp of the olive oil over a gentle heat, then add the onion and fry until soft, about 10 minutes. Add the garlic and chillies and fry for 1 minute or so, until the garlic releases its aroma, then add the tomatoes and the barbecue sauce. Stir everything, cover and cook for around 1 hour over a low heat, stirring frequently, until thickened. Season to taste with salt and pepper.

2. Preheat the oven to 180°C/350°F/gas 4.

3. Meanwhile, brush both sides of the aubergine slices with the remaining olive oil. Heat a griddle pan over a high heat and griddle the slices (in batches) until they are soft and have a few nice blackened and caramelised spots. Sprinkle them on both sides with the spice rub.

4. Begin to layer up the parmigiana: spoon a layer of the tomato sauce into a deep ovenproof dish, then top with a layer of spiced aubergine slices, mozzarella and a sprinkling of Parmesan. Repeat these layers as many times as the dish and ingredients allow, finishing with a layer of tomato sauce and a good sprinkling of mozzarella and Parmesan. This will pool out into a glorious puddle and crisp up to form a golden-brown crust.

5. Bake for 30–40 minutes until the crust looks good and a knife poked into the dish meets no resistance.

GREEN GODDESS PASTA SALAD

The creaminess of the avocado and the richness of the tahini makes this feel as though you're eating something quite naughty, when it's actually stuffed full of herbs and other good things that make this pasta salad pretty virtuous. This makes enough dukkah for another day – it will keep for a couple of months in an airtight container.

SERVES 6

500g (1lb 2oz) dried farfalle or other short pasta

1 tbsp olive oil

350g (12oz) baby plum or cherry tomatoes, halved

½ cucumber, finely diced

1 red onion, finely diced

115g (4oz) baby spinach

Dukkah:

50g (⅓ cup) hazelnuts, roughly chopped

2 tbsp sesame seeds

1 tbsp cumin seeds

1 tbsp fennel seeds

1 tbsp coriander seeds

3 tbsp pumpkin seeds

¼ tsp flaked sea salt

Dressing:

2 medium ripe avocados (about 200g/7oz in total)

4 tbsp Greek yoghurt

2 tbsp chopped tarragon

40g (2 cups) fresh coriander (cilantro) leaves

1½ tbsp tahini

120ml (½ cup) olive oil

1 garlic clove

1 tsp honey

juice of 1 lemon

salt and freshly ground black pepper, to taste

1. Preheat the oven to 180°C/350°F/gas 4.

2. Cook the pasta in a saucepan of boiling salted water according to the packet instructions. Drain, then dress with the olive oil and let cool, tossing occasionally to avoid sticking.

3. Put all of the dukkah ingredients except the pumpkin seeds and salt onto a baking tray (sheet) and bake in the oven until just golden brown and toasted, 8–10 minutes. Transfer to a mortar and pestle and lightly crush or pulse in a spice grinder a couple of times, then stir through the pumpkin seeds and salt.

4. Add all the dressing ingredients, except the seasoning, to a food processor and blitz until smooth. Season with salt and pepper to taste.

5. In a large bowl, mix together the cooled pasta with the tomatoes, cucumber, onion and spinach. Add the dressing and toss to coat evenly.

6. Serve with a sprinkling of dukkah.

CREAMY PEANUT BUTTER NOODLES

It's worth popping to a specialist Asian supermarket for these ingredients. Always worth the trip. Chinkiang vinegar has an amazing, sherry-like, malty smokiness that is hard to replicate (although a mixture of red wine and balsamic vinegars can come close); and Sichuan peppercorns bring an aromatic, numbing quality to the chilli oil, which is delicious. Serve either in a massive bowl in the middle of the table, or divide the dressing, chilli oil, noodles and garnishes between individual serving dishes and encourage your guests to mix up their own noodle bowls. PS – these are also delicious cold, and the dressing is 100% vegan.

SERVES 4

300g (10½oz) dried egg noodles
or other noodles

2 tsp sesame oil

Chilli oil:

2.5cm (1in) piece of fresh root
ginger, finely chopped

4 garlic cloves, finely chopped

4 tbsp Gochugaru or other mild red
pepper flakes

200ml (generous ¾ cup)
neutral oil

3–4 tbsp Sichuan peppercorns

whole spices, to taste, such as
a cinnamon stick, fennel seeds, star
anise or coriander seeds (optional)

Peanut butter dressing:

3 tbsp natural, unsweetened,
smooth peanut butter

1½ tbsp Chinese sesame paste
or tahini

3½ tbsp light soy sauce

2 tbsp Chinkiang
(Chinese black rice) vinegar

2 tsp maple syrup

4 tbsp hot vegetable stock
or hot water

To serve:

spring onion (scallion)
greens, thinly sliced

toasted sesame seeds

sliced cucumber

crushed, toasted peanuts

soft-boiled or fried eggs

1. First, make your chilli oil. Place the ginger, garlic and pepper flakes in a sturdy heatproof bowl and set aside.

2. Place the oil, Sichuan peppercorns and other whole spices (if using) in a small saucepan and place over a low flame. Cook gently for 15-20 minutes until aromatic. Watch the spices don't burn. Strain the oil and discard the fried spices, then return the oil to a medium-high heat. When hot, pour directly over the garlic, ginger and pepper flakes. Stir together until everything stops sizzling, then set aside to cool.

3. To make the dressing, whisk together the peanut butter, sesame paste, soy sauce, vinegar, maple syrup and hot stock or water. It should be smooth, slick and very flavoursome. Transfer the dressing to a large serving bowl and top with about two thirds of the chilli oil and its tasty bits. There should be an even film of red oil covering the dressing.

4. Cook your noodles according to the packet instructions, then drain and pour over the contents of a just-boiled kettle (this will rid them of excess starch and keep them hot. If you want to serve them cold, rinse under cold running water).

5. Dress the noodles with the sesame oil then tip into the middle of the oil-topped dressing. Cover in spring onion greens, toasted sesame seeds or any other garnishes of your choosing. Mix thoroughly and serve with the rest of the chilli oil on the side.

VEGAN MUSHROOM CARBONARA

It can sometimes be difficult to convince really dedicated carnivores that vegan dishes can be just as full of flavour as their meaty cousins. This carbonara recipe makes a persuasive argument; the creaminess from the cashews mixed with the miso is uncannily like a Parmesan sauce, and the mushrooms provide a similar meaty saltiness to the guanciale in the original Roman version.

SERVES 4

110g (1 cup) raw cashews, soaked for at least 3 hours in room temperature water, then drained

2 tbsp olive oil

200g (7oz) fresh shiitake mushrooms, thinly sliced

350g (12oz) dried linguine

1 tbsp brown miso paste

1 tsp lemon juice

100ml (generous ⅓ cup) oat (or other plant-based) milk

salt and freshly ground black pepper

1. Preheat the oven to 180°C/350°F/gas 4.

2. Put the soaked cashews into a saucepan of fresh cold water and bring to the boil. Reduce the heat and simmer for 10 minutes, then turn off the heat and let sit for a further 10 minutes before draining. Set aside.

3. Heat the olive oil in a large heavy pan over a medium heat and fry the mushrooms until they've lost most of their moisture and have begun to crisp up. Remove the pan from the heat.

4. Cook the linguine in a large saucepan of boiling salted water, according to the packet instructions. Drain, reserving around 150ml (⅔ cup) of the cooking water.

5. Meanwhile, add the drained cashews to a high-speed blender (preferably a Nutribullet), along with the miso, lemon juice, oat milk and plenty of black pepper. Blend to a smooth paste.

6. Toss the paste through the cooked pasta and mushrooms, adding splashes of the reserved starchy pasta water to make a creamy sauce (you probably won't need the whole amount to get a good consistency).

 ## Virgin green tea mojito p.41

Tea can be easily overshadowed in cocktails, so it's important to brew it for a while – a good five minutes should do.

SERVES 4

25–30 mint leaves, plus extra to garnish

400ml (scant 1¾ cups) strongly brewed green tea, strained and chilled (loose leaf is best for this – we like the sencha variety)

175ml (¾ cup) demerara syrup (see method step 1)

100ml (generous ⅓ cup) fresh lime juice (from 4–5 limes)

4 scoops ice cubes

soda water, to top up (optional)

lime wedges, to garnish

Demerara syrup:
225g (generous 1 cup) demerara (turbinado) sugar

250ml (generous 1 cup) water

1. For the syrup, heat the sugar and water in a small saucepan until the sugar has fully dissolved. Pour into a container and chill in the refrigerator until ready to use.

2. Lightly clap the mint leaves between your palms to release the oils, then place in a large serving jug (pitcher).

3. Pour in the tea, measured chilled demerara syrup and lime juice followed by the ice and stir well to combine.

4. Taste and top up with soda water (if using), giving it a final stir to combine.

5. Pour into individual glasses and garnish with sprigs of mint and wedges of lime.

Dinner Party

Dining with Dalí

A man obsessed with all things edible, Salvador Dalí threw dinner parties that were the talk of twentieth-century high society. At the artist's table, guests could expect to enjoy dishes as diverse as 'frog pasties', 'toffee with pinecones' or 'bush of crayfish in Viking herbs', while their host set about encouraging behaviour that was simultaneously 'sensual, imaginative and exotic'. All the excess was laid out in glorious detail in Dalí's infamous cookbook, *Les Dîners de Gala*.

**CONFIT CHICKEN
FATTEH**
48

**CARROT CAKE-
BOTTOMED
CHEESECAKE**
50

**40 CLOVES CONFIT
CHICKEN**
52

**MINI STEAK
WELLINGTONS &
PEPPERCORN SAUCE**
53

**NO-CHURN
CARAMEL POPCORN
ICE CREAM**
54

**ESPRESSO MARTINI
CAFETIÈRE**
54

**BAKED TARTIFLETTE
GNOCCHI**
57

**SLOW-COOKED
GOCHUJANG
SHORT RIBS**
58

**CHICKEN &
MUSHROOM
CASSOULET**
61

CONFIT CHICKEN FATTEH

Ah, the fatteh (or fattah, fattet, fetté, fata). A complex, layered dish featuring several components, it results in one of the most awesome mouthfuls of food there is. Its origins are hard to pin down, as there are derivations (things loaded onto pieces of bread with sauce) all over the Levant and indeed the world. Fatteh literally means 'broken pieces' or 'crumbs', which denotes the crispbread at the base of the dish. In Hama, Syria (and London!), the inclusion of a rice pilaf makes it more substantial – and the perfect dish for a special occasion. This is also amazing with roasted or poached chicken, and for breakfast the next day.

SERVES 6

4 white pitta breads, split in half

4 confit chicken legs **(p.52)**

Pilaf:

100g (scant ½ cup) unsalted butter, plus extra, melted, for brushing

3 red onions, thinly sliced into half-moons

500g (scant 3 cups) basmati rice

1 tsp black peppercorns

2 tsp allspice berries

3cm (1in) piece of cinnamon stick

3 cloves

50g (⅓ cup) sultanas (golden raisins)

125g (¾ cup) canned, drained chickpeas (garbanzo beans)

600ml (2½ cups) chicken stock

60g (2oz) flat-leaf parsley, finely chopped (a few sprigs reserved for garnish)

20g (¾oz) dill, finely chopped (a few sprigs reserved for garnish)

salt, to taste

Tomato sauce:

½ x Everything Garlicky Tomato Sauce recipe **(p.26)**

5cm (2in) piece of cinnamon stick

Yoghurt sauce:

300g (scant 1½ cups) thick Greek yoghurt

½ garlic clove, crushed to a paste

salt, to taste

Brown butter with pine nuts:

125g (generous ½ cup) butter, cubed

60g (½ cup) pine nuts

1. For the tomato sauce, halve and follow the recipe on **p.26,** adding the stick of cinnamon to the oil at the start. Remove the cinnamon stick, blend the sauce and set aside.

2. Melt the butter for the pilaf in a large, heavy saucepan (with a tight-fitting lid) over a low heat and add the sliced onions with a good pinch of salt. Cook very slowly, stirring only occasionally, for about 1 hour until the onions have collapsed and are rich and dark in colour.

3. Meanwhile, carefully but thoroughly wash the rice in a few changes of water until it runs clear, then cover with tepid water and leave to soak for 1 hour.

4. In a pestle and mortar, grind the black peppercorns, allspice berries, cinnamon stick and cloves to a powder. Reserve 1 tsp and tip the remaining mixture into the pan with the onions. Add the sultanas and chickpeas and cook for 2–3 minutes until the spices are fragrant.

5. Thoroughly drain the rice and add to the pan. Increase the heat a little and stir to gently coat the rice with the hot butter. When you can hear sizzling from the bottom of the pan, pour in the chicken stock, season with salt and tuck any rogue grains of rice below the surface of the liquid. Cover with a circle of greaseproof paper and put on the lid (do this as quickly as possible). Turn the heat to its highest setting and cook for 3½ minutes, then turn the heat right down and cook for a further 7 minutes. Remove from the heat and leave to stand for 15 minutes.

6. Meanwhile, preheat the oven to 160°C/325°F/gas 3.

7. Brush the pitta breads liberally with melted butter and bake in the oven until evenly browned and very crisp.

8. For the brown butter, melt the butter in a small saucepan over a medium heat and cook until nutty and brown, then transfer to a bowl. Put the pine nuts onto a baking tray and toast in the oven for 1–2 minutes, then tip into the butter.

9. Sprinkle the confit chicken legs with the reserved 1 tsp of spice mix. Roast, fry or grill (broil) for 10 minutes according to the instructions on **p.52**, then remove the meat from the bones, leaving a few larger pieces here and there.

10. Mix together the yoghurt sauce ingredients and loosen with some cold water. Warm through the tomato sauce.

11. Build your fatteh. Crack the crisp pitta breads into bite-size pieces and spread over a large platter. Fluff the rice pilaf with a fork, fold in the chopped herbs and transfer it to the platter. Scatter over the crispy confit chicken, then dress with the warm tomato sauce, yoghurt sauce, brown butter and pine nuts, and a few whole herbs. Get stuck in.

CARROT CAKE-BOTTOMED CHEESECAKE

Carrot cake is our favourite type of cake. A close second was cheesecake. Do the math.

SERVES 8

Carrot cake base:

150ml (⅔ cup) vegetable oil

125g (scant ⅔ cup) granulated sugar

85g (scant ½ cup) brown sugar

1 tsp vanilla extract

2 eggs

140g (generous 1 cup) plain (all-purpose) flour

½ tsp fine sea salt

1½ tsp baking powder

1 tsp ground cinnamon

¼ tsp ground nutmeg

165g (6oz) carrots, peeled and grated

Cheesecake:

40g (⅓ cup) chopped pecans, to decorate

370g (1¾ cups) double or whipping (heavy) cream

450g (2 cups) cream cheese, softened

185g (1½ cups) icing (confectioners') sugar, sifted

1 tsp vanilla extract

1. Preheat the oven to 180°C/350°F/gas 4. Grease and line a 23cm (9in) springform cake pan.

2. In a large bowl, whisk together the oil, sugars, vanilla extract and eggs until smooth. Sift in the flour, salt, baking powder, cinnamon and nutmeg and whisk until just combined. Fold in the grated carrots and scrape the mixture into the prepared pan.

3. Bake for 35–40 minutes, or until an inserted toothpick comes out clean. Set aside to cool completely.

4. Spread the pecans in an even layer over a baking tray and bake for about 10 minutes until golden brown and toasted (keep an eye on them so they toast evenly). Set aside to cool completely.

5. Using a hand mixer, whisk the cream in a large bowl until stiff peaks are formed. In a separate bowl, whisk together the cream cheese, icing sugar and vanilla extract. Fold the whipped cream into the cream cheese mixture until well combined, then spread the mixture on top of the carrot cake and smooth the surface with an angled spatula.

6. Chill in the refrigerator for 6 hours or overnight.

7. Sprinkle the chopped pecans around the edge of the cheesecake, then release the cheesecake from the pan and slide onto a cake stand or serving plate. Slice and serve!

40 CLOVES CONFIT CHICKEN

p.51

There are a few steps to this recipe and it takes a bit of time, so do source the very best chicken legs you can. Confit garlic gets a lot of press. Who does his PR?! Garlic press, get it? Anyway, we like to purée the confit garlic and add it to heavily buttered mashed potatoes. Great with the crispy chicken and (maybe) a salad. If you have any left over, do make the Confit Chicken Fatteh on **p.48**.

SERVES 4–6

4–6 top-quality chicken legs

44 (ish) garlic cloves: 4 roughly chopped; 40 peeled and left whole

20 thyme sprigs: 10 roughly chopped; 10 left whole

8 fresh bay leaves: 6 roughly chopped; 2 left whole

4–6 tbsp flaked sea salt

very coarsely ground black pepper

1.5l (6¼ cups) mild olive oil

1. Choose a dish or container large enough to fit your chicken legs snugly in one layer and sprinkle half of the chopped garlic, thyme and bay evenly over the bottom. Season the chicken legs very generously with the salt and pepper (about 1 tbsp flaked salt per leg), layer them on top of the aromatics, skin-side up, then cover with the remaining chopped aromatics. Wrap the tray in clingfilm (plastic wrap) and refrigerate overnight.

2. The next day, preheat the oven to 100°C/210°F/gas ¼.

3. Wash off any bits of marinade from the chicken legs and dry extremely well with kitchen paper. Using a sharp knife, cut around the base of each leg, being sure to sever the tendons by cutting right down to the bone. This keeps the confit looking neat and prevents the skin from tearing as it cooks.

4. Lay the legs, skin-side up, in the bottom of your widest, flameproof casserole dish, along with the whole garlic cloves, whole thyme sprigs and bay leaves. Try to keep everything in one layer. Pour over the olive oil and place the dish over a medium heat. As soon as the temperature of the oil reaches 97°C/206°F, or you see larger bubbles appear at the surface of the oil, transfer to the oven.

5. Cook (uncovered) for 2½–3 hours, or until the legs are very soft but still holding their shape. At this point the garlic should be outrageously sweet, darker in colour, dehydrated and almost chewy, but should not be burned or bitter-tasting. If at any point you are concerned about them colouring too much, or aren't using particularly fat cloves, feel free to fish them out and set aside until the chicken is ready.

6. If you are not planning to eat the confit immediately, leave to cool slightly, then carefully remove the chicken from the oil and place into a sterilised jar or container. Scoop the confit garlic cloves into a separate container and ladle over enough oil to cover. Strain the remaining fat over the chicken and discard the herbs. Both the chicken and the garlic will keep well in the refrigerator for up to 2 weeks.

7. To cook your confit, remove the desired amount of legs from the storage vessel and bring up to room temperature. Scrape off any excess fat then choose from the following: **a)** place skin-side up on a rack set over a baking tray and roast at 220°C/425°F/gas 7 for 10 minutes, or until crisp; or **b)** fry the legs, skin-side down, in a non-stick pan over a medium-low heat for 10 minutes, flipping onto the flesh side for a few further minutes. Drain briefly on kitchen paper, then serve.

8. Mash the confit garlic cloves through lots of heavily buttered mashed potatoes and serve alongside the crispy chicken legs.

MINI STEAK WELLINGTONS & PEPPERCORN SAUCE

 p.55

The true origins of the Beef Wellington are lost in the dark waters of history. Was it created to honour the Battle of Waterloo? Is it merely a British appropriation of the French filet de bœuf en croûte? Provenance aside, if the thought of splashing out on a piece of beef fillet makes you feel light-headed, try our delicious mini versions – a fraction of the price, much easier and soggy-bottom-free.

SERVES 4

2 tbsp unsalted butter

3 shallots, finely diced

500g (1lb 2oz) mixed mushrooms, very finely diced or pulsed in batches in a food processor

2 tbsp thyme leaves

100ml (generous ⅓ cup) white wine

1 tbsp vegetable oil

4 x small fillet steaks, about 4cm (1½in) thick

2 sheets of ready rolled, all-butter puff pastry (approx. 35 x 23cm/14 x 9in)

8 slices of Parma ham

2 eggs

salt and freshly ground black pepper, to taste

buttered greens, to serve

Peppercorn sauce:

40g (3 tbsp) unsalted butter

1 shallot, finely chopped

1 tbsp black peppercorns, coarsely ground

3½ tbsp brandy

150ml (⅔ cup) rich beef stock

150ml (⅔ cup) double (heavy) cream

1 tsp Dijon mustard

generous squeeze of lemon juice

salt, to taste

1. Heat the butter in a small frying pan (skillet) over a medium heat, add the shallots and mushrooms and fry until they have released all of their moisture and everything is dry. Add the thyme and the wine and continue to cook for about 5 minutes, stirring often, until you have a really rich, dense paste. Season to taste and set aside to cool.

2. Heat the vegetable oil in a large heavy frying pan until very hot, almost smoking. Season the steaks on each side with a little salt and pepper, then sear them on each side for 15–20 seconds, to get a little colour. Set aside to rest briefly. (If the steaks let off any juices, reserve to pour into the pan with the stock in step 7. Keep the pan unwashed to make the sauce later in the recipe).

3. Cut each sheet of puff pastry widthways into 2 rectangles. Spread about 3 tbsp of the cooled mushroom paste over each piece of pastry, leaving a border of about 1cm (½in) clear around the edges, then top each with 2 slices of the Parma ham and place the fillet steaks on top in the middle. Wrap the ham around the steaks to enclose.

4. Beat the eggs in a small bowl with a little water and a pinch of salt. Brush the pastry edges with the egg wash, then fold the pastry in half over each steak to enclose, pressing down around the edges to seal well. Trim each parcel to form a semicircle around the steak, then crimp or pinch the edges to achieve a rim. Chill the wellingtons in the refrigerator for 20 minutes.

5. Meanwhile, preheat the oven to 240°C/475°F/gas 9. Place a baking tray in the oven to heat up.

6. Brush the chilled wellingtons with the egg wash and place on the preheated baking tray. Bake for 12–15 minutes until the puff pastry is golden and puffed up. Remove from the oven and let rest for 10 minutes.

7. Meanwhile, make the sauce. Heat the butter in the steak pan over a medium heat, add the shallot and sweat for about 5 minutes until soft. Add the crushed peppercorns and toast for around 30 seconds, then add the brandy to deglaze the pan. Pour in the beef stock, reduce briefly, then pour in the cream and stir in the mustard. Cook very gently for a few more minutes, to marry the flavours, then add lemon juice and salt, to taste.

8. Serve the mini wellingtons with the sauce and some buttered greens.

NO-CHURN CARAMEL POPCORN ICE CREAM

The trick with our ice cream is that, ingeniously, it calls for cream, simply whipped to achieve the right texture, replacing the tedious churning of custard that ice cream makers usually have to put up with. The cream itself can be infused with all sorts of flavours, but that nutty moreishness of popcorn suits this recipe brilliantly.

SERVES 4

600ml (2½ cups) double (heavy) cream

a large handful (¾ cup) salted popcorn

1 x 400g (14oz) can condensed milk

100g (⅓ cup) salted caramel sauce, plus extra to decorate

toffee popcorn, to serve

1. Heat the cream in a saucepan over a medium heat until warmed through, then remove from the heat and submerge the popcorn in the cream. Set aside to infuse for 30–45 minutes.

2. Strain the cream into a bowl through a fine mesh sieve or a colander lined with cheesecloth (muslin) and transfer to the refrigerator to completely cool. Discard the steeped popcorn.

3. Combine the cooled cream and condensed milk in a blender and process until thoroughly combined. Pour into a freezerproof container and swirl through the caramel with a knife or skewer.

4. Cover and freeze for 6–8 hours, or overnight for best results, until set.

5. Serve decorated with toffee popcorn and drizzled with extra caramel sauce.

 Espresso Martini Cafetière

Espresso Martinis, generally, are expected to be frothy affairs – something we didn't want you to miss out on at home. Your cafetière isn't just for coffee, you know!

SERVES 4

225ml (scant 1 cup) freshly brewed strong coffee

120ml (½ cup) coffee liqueur

200ml (generous ¾ cup) vodka

cubed ice, to serve (optional)

1. Allow the coffee to cool, then pour into a large mixing jug (pitcher), along with the coffee liqueur and vodka. Chill the mixture in the refrigerator for at least 30 minutes, or until ready to serve.

2. Pour the mixture into a clean, sturdy cafetière and use the plunger to beat the mixture repeatedly, until a considerable foamy 'head' has developed.

3. Immediately pour into individual glasses over cubed ice.

BAKED TARTIFLETTE GNOCCHI

Despite being world-famous and a firm feature on apres-ski menus throughout the Alpine resorts of the Haute-Savoie, Tartiflette has a deceptively brief history. Hit by flailing sales of their beloved Reblochon cheese in the 1980s, the French came up with the dish in an attempt to shift a few more units. Marketing has never tasted so good, huh? We imagine our version, which features crispy fried pillowy potato gnocchi, being enjoyed by climbers on the top of Mont Blanc, at the Franco-Italian border, to celebrate making it to the top. If you haven't just scaled a mountain, you may need to go for a walk afterwards.

SERVES 4–6

1kg (2lb 3oz) large floury baking potatoes (to yield about 800g/1lb 12oz potato flesh)

2 large egg yolks, beaten

200g (1½ cups) plain (all-purpose) flour, plus extra for dusting

2 tbsp olive oil, plus extra for greasing

150g (5½oz) Reblochon (or Delice du Jura), thinly sliced

fine sea salt, for the baking tray

Sauce:

300g (10½oz) round shallots, peeled but left whole

1 tbsp olive oil

1 tsp sugar

150g (5½oz) bacon lardons

1 tbsp unsalted butter, plus extra for frying (optional)

2 garlic cloves, finely chopped

a handful of sage leaves, plus extra for garnish (optional)

100ml (generous ⅓ cup) dry white wine

1 tbsp white wine vinegar

150ml (⅔ cup) chicken stock

150ml (⅔ cup) double (heavy) cream

salt and freshly ground black pepper, to taste

1. Preheat the oven to 200°C/400°F/gas 6.

2. Spread a thin layer of salt over a baking tray and arrange the baking potatoes on top. Bake them in the oven for 1 hour 20 minutes, or until easily pierced with a knife.

3. Meanwhile, toss the shallots for the sauce in the oil, sugar and a pinch of salt, place on a separate baking tray and roast for about 30 minutes until soft, sweet and caramelised. Set aside to cool.

4. Remove the potatoes from the oven and let cool for 10 minutes or so, then split them and cradle the halves in a cloth as you spoon the flesh out into a bowl. While still hot, pass the flesh through a potato ricer directly onto a clean work surface. Sprinkle evenly with 1 tsp sea salt and, when they have stopped steaming but are still warm, drizzle over the egg yolk. Sift over the flour, then use a bench scraper (or a large knife) to vertically chop the flour into the potato until the flour is evenly distributed and the mixture looks like lots of little pebbles. At this point, bring the dough together with your hands by gently kneading a few times. Don't overwork it or it will become either gluey or chewy, neither of which are pleasant.

5. Dust the work surface with flour, cut the dough into 4 chunks and roll out into fat sausages. Chop these into 2cm (¾in) thick rounds and set aside, loosely covered with some clingfilm (plastic wrap).

6. Bring a large saucepan of well salted water to the boil and lightly oil a baking tray. Working in batches, drop your gnocchi into the boiling water and simmer until they float to the surface, roughly 2 minutes. When they float, wait 20 seconds or so, then remove with a slotted spoon and transfer to the oiled tray.

7. Place a large, non-stick sauté pan over a medium-high heat and add the olive oil. When hot, add a third of the gnocchi and fry until crisp and golden on both sides, 2–3 minutes. Repeat with the remaining 2 batches and set aside.

8. Wipe out the pan with kitchen paper and reduce the heat to medium. Add the bacon lardons and fry until golden and the fat has rendered, about 5 minutes. Add the butter, chopped garlic and sage leaves and cook until fragrant (watch the garlic doesn't brown), then add the wine and vinegar and cook for about 3 minutes, until reduced by half. Add the stock and cook for about 5 minutes, until reduced by half again, then pour in the cream. Cut the roasted shallots in half and add to the sauce, then season with plenty of salt and pepper to taste. Finally, stir in the fried gnocchi.

9. Meanwhile, preheat the grill (broiler) to high.

10. Transfer the mixture to an ovenproof dish, ensuring that everything is evenly distributed. Layer over the Reblochon slices and grill for a few minutes, until golden brown and bubbling. If you like, fry a few more sage leaves in a little butter until crisp and arrange over the top. Enjoy!

SLOW-COOKED GOCHUJANG SHORT RIBS

Gochujang is a Korean hot-sweet fermented pepper paste – for cooks it is an awesome thing. More commonly used as a condiment for your bibimbap, here it is cooked slowly with fatty short ribs, imparting a deep crimson hue and an ethereal funk to the gravy. Make sure to look for the pastes that come in the red, treasure-box-like tubs – the others are often poor imitations. Delicious eaten with sticky rice, kimchi or a crunchy salad.

SERVES 4–6

2kg (4lb 6oz) beef short ribs (bone-in), at room temperature

groundnut oil, for frying

2 onions, cut into large chunks

3 fat slices of fresh root ginger

6 fat garlic cloves, smashed but left whole

150ml (⅔ cup) Shaoxing rice wine or dry sherry

120g (⅓ cup) gochujang (Korean hot pepper paste)

2 tbsp light soy sauce

1 tbsp dark soy sauce

4 tbsp Chinkiang (Chinese black rice) vinegar or rice wine vinegar

3 tbsp brown sugar

salt and freshly ground black pepper

To serve:

1 tbsp sesame oil

1 tbsp cornflour (cornstarch), mixed with a little water

toasted sesame seeds, for sprinkling

spring onion (scallion) greens, sliced

1. Preheat the oven to 150°C/300°F/gas 2 and place a large, flameproof casserole dish over a medium heat.

2. Pat the short-ribs dry with kitchen paper and season half of the ribs well with salt and pepper.

3. Cover the bottom of the casserole dish with groundnut oil and, when hot, brown the seasoned ribs for 10-15 minutes until you have achieved good colour on all sides. Be careful not to let the casserole get too hot – you don't want to singe the meat or burn any solids on the bottom. Remove the browned ribs along with any excess oil, then season and brown the second batch of ribs. Set aside with the others.

4. Add the onion, ginger and garlic to the casserole to cook in the same oil. As soon as everything is starting to take on some colour, stir in the rice wine followed by all the remaining ingredients. Return the browned ribs to the dish and add enough water to just cover all the meat. Cover the surface of the liquid with a circle of greaseproof paper and partially cover the casserole with a lid (leaving a gap of about 3cm/1in). Cook in the oven for 3½–4 hours, or until the meat is very soft and falling from the bone.

5. Remove from the oven and let cool briefly, then discard the greaseproof paper. Carefully transfer the ribs from the sauce to a container (in one layer), cover and set aside. When the sauce in the casserole is cool, strain it into another vessel, discarding the aromatics, and place in the freezer to allow the fat to separate and solidify. When cold, lift out the bright orange fat with a slotted spoon (or your hands) and discard.

6. To serve, place the ribs back in the oven for 10–15 minutes to heat through.

7. Place the sauce into a saucepan with the sesame oil and cook over a medium heat until reduced by half, 5–10 minutes. It should be very rich and glossy. Whisk in the cornflour paste.

8. Arrange the hot ribs on a large serving platter, then lacquer with the gravy before sprinkling liberally with sesame seeds and spring onions.

CHICKEN & MUSHROOM CASSOULET

Cassoulet is one of the world's great dishes – a true paean to hearty French peasant nosh. Ours uses our Confit Chicken (see **p.52**) in place of the traditional duck, and is a (slightly) slimmed down version, sans pigs' feet. It is full of the earthiness of porcini, the richness of stock and the creaminess of haricot (navy) beans and is best enjoyed with green salad and a hearty French red.

SERVES 4–6

30g (1oz) dried porcini mushrooms

2 tbsp olive oil

1 tbsp unsalted butter

4 large good-quality sausages, preferably Toulouse

150g (1 cup) unsmoked bacon lardons

2 medium brown onions, diced

300g (10½oz) oyster mushrooms

5 garlic cloves, crushed

2 plum tomatoes (from a can)

5 thyme sprigs

1 bay leaf

100ml (generous ⅓ cup) white wine

400ml (1¾ cups) good-quality chicken stock

3 x 400g (14oz) cans haricot (navy) beans, drained and rinsed

2 legs confit chicken (**p.52**) (alternatively, use fresh chicken thighs, seasoned and browned in oil)

salt and freshly ground black pepper, to taste

Topping:

100g (2⅓ cups) panko breadcrumbs

3 tbsp olive oil

1 tsp salt

1. Rehydrate the porcini mushrooms in 300ml (1¼ cups) warm water for around 1 hour, then remove, squeeze out excess water and chop into small pieces. Strain the mushroomy soaking water into a small measuring jug – you should have roughly 250ml (generous 1 cup).

2. Preheat the oven to 180°C/350°F/gas 4.

3. In a large, wide, flameproof casserole dish, heat 1 tbsp of the olive oil and the butter over a medium heat. Add the sausages and brown for around 5 minutes until coloured all over and almost cooked through. Remove, set aside and cut into chunks when cool enough to handle.

4. Add the bacon to the same pan and cook until crisp, then remove and set aside.

5. Add onions to the same pan and fry in the bacon fat over the gentlest heat for about 30 minutes until soft and sticky.

6. Add a little more oil to a separate pan and fry the mushrooms in batches until beginning to caramelise. Set aside with the sausages and bacon.

7. Add the garlic to the onions and fry for 1–2 minutes, until fragrant, then add the plum tomatoes, ripped up a bit with your fingers, the chopped porcini mushrooms, thyme and bay. Add the white wine to deglaze the pan.

8. Add the reserved mushroom broth and the chicken stock and simmer for around 10–15 minutes until reduced. Add the beans, then stir through the oyster mushrooms and bacon and season with salt and pepper. Add the cooked sausages, burying them deep in the liquid. Place the confit chicken legs (or thighs) on top, pressing them down into the beans. Transfer to the oven and bake, uncovered, for 30 minutes.

9. In a bowl, mix together the panko breadcrumbs and olive oil. Remove the casserole from the oven, scatter the panko mixture on top of the beans and return to the oven for a further 30 minutes until the breadcrumbs are golden and crisp and the sauce has thickened.

Picnic

Death is a Picnic

As unappetising as eating in a graveyard may sound, picnicking with
the dead has a long history. In nineteenth-century America, cemeteries
were seen as an ideal escape from the disease-ridden squalor of the city,
providing the perfect place for families to relax in the great outdoors.
The mouldering remains of the recently deceased were, apparently,
neither here nor there.

'PHILIPPE DUBOIS' CHICKEN TIKKA BAGUETTES

Philippe Dubois was an unassuming and decidedly un-French caff in Birmingham, England that specialised in progressive baguette fillings. This is our version of their most popular offering, which you could order hot or cold with a side of cheap, salty crisps.

SERVES 4

Chicken tikka:

3cm (1in) piece of fresh root ginger

4 garlic cloves

150g (¾ cup) thick, strained Greek yoghurt

1 tsp Kashmiri (mild) chilli powder

½ tsp ground turmeric

½ tsp garam masala

1 tsp smoked paprika

1½ tsp ground cumin

1½ tsp ground coriander

¼ tsp ground cinnamon

1 tbsp flaked salt

2 tbsp lemon juice

600g (1lb 5oz) chicken breasts (about 4), cut into bite-size chunks

50g (3½ tbsp) unsalted butter, melted

Tikka paste:

1 tbsp neutral oil

½ tsp cumin seeds

½ onion, finely chopped

1 tbsp tomato purée

¼ tsp Kashmiri (mild) chilli powder

¼ tsp smoked paprika

½ tsp ground cumin

½ tsp ground coriander

¼ tsp ground turmeric

salt, to taste

Sandwich filler:

100g (scant ½ cup) mayonnaise

50g (¼ cup) thick Greek yoghurt

a small handful of coriander (cilantro), finely chopped

2 tsp good mango chutney, or to taste

a squeeze of lemon juice, to taste

To serve:

cheap salted crisps (chips)

freshly ground black pepper

crusty French baguettes, split

sliced cucumber

shredded iceberg lettuce

1. For the chicken tikka, crush the ginger and garlic to a paste in a pestle and mortar, then scoop into a bowl along with all the other ingredients (apart from the melted butter). Mix thoroughly, then cover and leave to marinate at room temperature for at least 1 hour.

2. To make the tikka paste, heat the oil in a small saucepan over a medium heat and, when hot, add the cumin seeds. When they crackle, add the onion and a small pinch of salt. Cook for about 10 minutes until the onion is golden brown, then add the tomato purée and cook out briefly before tipping in the ground spices. Remove from the heat to cool.

3. Preheat the grill (broiler) to high.

4. Slide the marinated chicken pieces onto a few skewers, then suspend them across an ovenproof baking dish or a cast-iron pan. Grill (broil) for 10–15 minutes, turning halfway through and basting occasionally with the melted butter, until cooked through and a little charred. Let cool slightly, then slice the chicken off the skewers into rough pieces and transfer to a bowl to cool completely.

5. Fold the tikka paste through the cooled chicken, along with the mayonnaise, yoghurt, coriander, chutney and lemon juice, to taste. Load into a container for the picnic.

6. When ready to eat, crack open your packets of crisps, grind in lots of black pepper and shake them really well. Load the chicken tikka sandwich filler into the baguettes along with a fistful of crisps, some fat wedges of cucumber and some shredded lettuce. Enjoy!

CAPONATA MOZZARELLA SANDWICHES

Caponata (a Sicilian stew, of sorts) is hugely versatile, but is delicious in a sandwich. If you have the wherewithal, make it the day before you want to eat your sandwiches. As with lots of dishes, a long rest allows for the flavours to round out and further marry. We've added some good buffalo mozzarella for muscle. A couple of good salted anchovy fillets wouldn't go amiss either.

SERVES 4–6

2 small aubergines (eggplants)

3 celery sticks, trimmed and sliced on an angle into 1cm (½in) chunks

4 tbsp good olive oil, plus extra for dressing

neutral oil, for deep-frying

2 red onions, sliced into half-moons

2 fat garlic cloves, thinly sliced

1 x 400g (14oz) can whole plum tomatoes, drained

2 tbsp salted capers, rinsed and drained

50g (½ cup) black olives, pitted and torn

2 tbsp white sugar

4 tbsp red wine vinegar

40g (generous ¼ cup) pine nuts, toasted

a handful of basil leaves

salt, to taste

To serve:

1 x Rosemary & Garlic Focaccia (p.21)

2 x good-quality buffalo mozzarella balls

sea salt flakes, to taste

1. Cut the aubergines into 3cm (1in) chunks. Toss well with some salt and place in a colander or sieve to drain for 1 hour.

2. Meanwhile, bring a saucepan of very well salted water to the boil, add the celery and blanch until tender to the bite, 2–3 minutes. Drain, dress with a little olive oil and set aside.

3. Thoroughly rinse the aubergines under running water, then pat very dry with kitchen paper.

4. Heat a 5cm (2in) depth of oil in a deep, heavy saucepan to 175ºC (350ºF). Working in batches, fry the aubergine pieces until golden brown, about 5 minutes. Drain on kitchen paper and set aside.

5. In another saucepan, heat the 4 tbsp olive oil over a medium heat, add the onions and fry until they are translucent and have collapsed a little, but are not browned. Push them to one side and allow the oil to run to the other side of the pan. Reduce the heat a little, add the garlic and fry until sticky but not coloured, then chuck in the blanched celery and stir to incorporate.

6. Turn the heat back up to medium. Crush the drained tomatoes in your hands and add to the pan with a small pinch of salt. Cook for 10 minutes or so, stirring often to make sure nothing catches, then add the capers, olives, sugar and vinegar. Cook for another 1 minute or so to marry the flavours and dissolve the sugar, then remove from the heat. Stir through the fried aubergines, pine nuts and basil and allow to cool.

7. Transfer to a container and drizzle with a little more olive oil. Get off to the park!

8. Slice your focaccia in half and load with the caponata. Tear over the mozzarella and sprinkle with a little flaked salt. Get stuck in.

BANH MI SAUSAGE ROLLS

p.67

The Banh Mi is, without doubt, one of the world's greatest sandwiches – a sublime blend of East meets West and a rare example of a good thing that came from Western colonisation. We took the flavours of this perfect sarnie and put them in a sausage roll (we love sausage rolls). The flavours work deliciously together – pork, lemongrass, fish sauce and that mysterious secret ingredient, Maggi Seasoning.

SERVES 6

170g (6oz) fresh white bread, ripped into pieces

900g (2lb) minced (ground) pork

4 garlic cloves, very finely crushed

6cm (2½in) stalk of fresh lemongrass, very finely chopped

4cm (1½in) piece of fresh root ginger, very finely chopped

1 tbsp chilli flakes

1 tsp fennel seeds, toasted and crushed

1 tsp coriander seeds, toasted

1½ tsp freshly ground black pepper

2 tbsp soft brown sugar

1 tbsp flaked sea salt

1 tsp Maggi Liquid Seasoning

1 tsp fish sauce

500g (1lb 2oz) ready-made all-butter puff pastry

1 egg, beaten with a little milk

1 tsp white sesame seeds

1 tsp black sesame seeds

1. Preheat the oven to 180°C/350°F/gas 4. Line a baking tray with greaseproof paper.

2. Pop the bread into a food processor and blitz to fine breadcrumbs, then transfer to a large bowl. Add the pork to the breadcrumbs and mix through with your hands. Add the garlic, lemongrass, ginger, chilli flakes, fennel seeds, coriander seeds, black pepper, sugar, salt, Maggi Seasoning and fish sauce and mix until well combined.

3. Roll out the pastry to about 5mm (¼in) thick and roughly 50 x 30cm (20 x 12in).

4. Form the sausagemeat into a long, even sausage shape about 50cm (20in) long (the same length as the pastry) and place it on top of the pastry. Brush the exposed pastry with egg wash, then roll the pastry over the sausagemeat to enclose and crimp the join together with a fork. Brush the whole log with egg wash and sprinkle both types of sesame seeds over the top. Cut into 6 sausage rolls and place on the baking tray.

5. Bake for around 40 minutes until golden and cooked through. Use a meat thermometer if you have one – the meat in the middle should be 71°C (160°F).

PASTA SALAD ALLA NORMA

p.70

Sicilians are at loggerheads tracing the true origins of pasta 'alla norma', from which our salad takes inspiration. Some say it was created as an ode to the famous Catanian, Vincenzo Bellini, and the beauty of his opera, Norma. Others say that the constituent ingredients of the dish symbolise elements of the local terroir, and that of Mount Etna specifically. The tomato sauce is the lava, while the salted ricotta represents the snowfall during the winter months. Whatever you believe, believe this: pasta salad is back.

SERVES 4–6

Oven-dried tomatoes:

400g (14oz) baby plum tomatoes, halved

1 tsp fine sea salt

1 tsp caster (superfine) sugar

Salad:

2 firm, medium aubergines (eggplants)

1 tbsp fine sea salt

groundnut oil, for frying

500g (1lb 2oz) dried penne rigate

about 3½ tbsp good-quality olive oil

½ garlic clove, finely grated

2 tbsp red wine vinegar

½ red onion, very finely chopped

60g (½ cup) pine nuts, toasted

120g (4½oz) feta, crumbled

a large handful of basil, torn (or more if omitting the oregano)

a small handful of fresh oregano, roughly chopped (optional)

salt and freshly ground black pepper, to taste

1. Preheat the oven to 120°C/250°F/gas ½.

2. Place the tomatoes, cut-side up, on a large baking tray. Combine the salt with the sugar, then sprinkle evenly over the tomatoes (you shouldn't need all of it). Bake for about 3 hours, or until dried out and deliciously sweet (the time it takes will depend on the size of your tomatoes). Remove from the oven and let cool. You can store these in oil in the refrigerator until you're ready to use them, if you like.

3. Cut the aubergines into 2cm (¾in) chunks. Sprinkle with the fine sea salt and toss very thoroughly, then place in a colander to drain for 1 hour. Rinse well with water, then pat completely dry with kitchen paper.

4. Heat a 3cm (1in) depth of oil in a deep, heavy saucepan over a medium heat to 175°C (350°F). Fry the aubergine pieces in two batches until crisp and golden brown. Remove with a slotted spoon to drain on kitchen paper and set aside.

5. Bring a large saucepan of salted water to the boil, add the pasta and cook according to the packet instructions. Drain and dress the pasta with a little olive oil, then set aside to cool, stirring occasionally to avoid sticking.

6. In a large mixing bowl, combine the remaining olive oil with the garlic, vinegar, a pinch of sea salt and a generous amount of freshly ground black pepper. Add the red onion and pine nuts, followed by the pasta, oven-dried tomatoes, fried aubergines, feta, basil and oregano (if using). Toss well, adding a little more oil if you feel it needs it. Load into picnic tubs and get off to the park.

SRIRACHA DEVILLED EGG BLT

Sriracha is brilliant with eggs, hence its ever-presence at brunch tables around the world. This is a delicious sandwich.

SERVES 4

8 large eggs

3 tbsp sriracha hot sauce

120g (½ cup) mayonnaise

1 tsp mustard powder

½ tsp celery salt, or to taste

3 tbsp finely chopped fresh coriander (cilantro)

3 tbsp finely chopped chives

2 tbsp finely chopped fresh mint

zest and juice of ½ lime

To serve:

1 large ciabatta loaf, halved lengthways and sliced into 4

lettuce leaves (butterhead/ romaine/iceberg)

2 nice tomatoes, sliced and seasoned with a little salt

12 smoked streaky bacon rashers, cooked until very crisp

1 hot red chilli, sliced

1. To cook your eggs, bring a large shallow pan of water to a light simmer and carefully lower in your eggs. Cook for 10 minutes, then drain and drop into a large bowl of iced water and allow the eggs to cool completely, about 10 minutes.

2. Peel the eggs, cut in half and scoop out the yolks into the bowl of a food processor, reserving the whites. To the yolks, add the sriracha, mayonnaise, mustard powder and celery salt. Process until smooth, then add the herbs, lime zest and juice and process again until well incorporated. Add the reserved egg whites and pulse just a couple of times to keep the egg whites nice and chunky.

3. Toast the bread, then load with lettuce, tomatoes, the devilled egg mixture, crispy bacon and red chilli. Wrap up and get to the park.

 ## Raspberry prosecco mojito jug

Other than, perhaps, a Campari Spritz, we couldn't think of a better cocktail to spend a day in the park with.

SERVES 4

20–25 mint leaves, plus extra to garnish

200ml (generous ¾ cup) white rum

75ml (⅓ cup) lime juice

150ml (⅔ cup) raspberry syrup (see step 1 of method)

ice cubes

a handful of fresh raspberries

200ml (generous ¾ cup) prosecco, chilled

Raspberry syrup:

225g (generous 1 cup) caster (superfine) sugar

250g (scant 2 cups) fresh raspberries

250ml (generous 1 cup) water

1. For the syrup, bring the sugar, raspberries and water to the boil in a small saucepan, stirring until the raspberries have broken down and the sugar has dissolved. Strain by pushing as much of the pulp as possible through a sieve, then chill in the refrigerator until ready to serve.

2. Lightly clap the mint leaves between your palms to release the oils, then place in a large serving jug (pitcher). Pour in the rum, lime juice and measured raspberry syrup and stir to combine.

3. Add ice and fresh raspberries then top the lot up with the prosecco. Give the whole thing a stir and serve in individual glasses with more ice and garnished with mint.

ROAST CHICKEN, TOMATO & TARRAGON AIOLI SANDWICHES

This is probably the best sandwich in the world. It's best to roast the chicken fresh for this, rather than using yesterday's leftovers. The crisp skin and the resting juices make the world of difference.

SERVES 6

Tarragon aioli:

2 large fresh egg yolks

1 tbsp Dijon mustard

1 tsp white wine vinegar

1 tsp lemon juice

2 fat garlic cloves, crushed

200ml (generous ¾ cup) neutral oil

50ml (3½ tbsp) olive oil

2 tbsp finely chopped tarragon

salt and freshly ground black pepper, to taste

Shoestring fries:

1–2 large, floury potatoes (Maris Piper or King Edward are good)

groundnut oil, for deep-frying

flaked sea salt, to taste

Sandwiches:

2 French baguettes, each cut into 3

lettuce leaves (optional)

2–3 posh, ripe tomatoes, sliced and seasoned with a little salt

1 x Foil-Ball Roast Chicken (p.213), preferably still warm, shredded

1. To make the tarragon aioli, follow the method for Stick Blender Mayo (p.26), replacing the English mustard with Dijon mustard and adding crushed garlic to the base. Once transferred to the bowl, stir through the tarragon and lots of black pepper. Check for salt and leave to sit a while before you build your sandwich.

2. For the shoestring fries, wash your potato(es) well, leaving the skin on, then cut into fat matchsticks using a fluted mandoline cutter (or a spiralizer, or even by hand!). Rinse the potato matchsticks well, then dunk into a big bowl of cold water and let sit for 10 minutes. Drain and dry very thoroughly with kitchen paper.

3. Heat the oil in a deep, heavy saucepan to 175°C (350°F). Working in 2 or 3 batches, deep-fry the potato matchsticks until lightly golden brown and there is very little activity in the oil surrounding the fries. Lift out with a slotted spoon, drain briefly on kitchen paper and toss with a little flaked sea salt.

4. Schmear the baguettes with loads of tarragon aioli, layer over some lettuce and tomatoes, then stuff in as much roast chicken (and skin!) and shoestring fries as you can. Wrap the sandwiches up in baking parchment and head out into the sunshine.

TWO GREAT HAM SANDWICHES

There are ham sandwiches, and then there are ham sandwiches.

SERVES 6

The ham (makes lots):

2kg (4lb 6oz) bone-in ham hocks

1 large onion, halved

2 celery sticks

1 bunch of flat-leaf parsley stalks

1 tbsp black peppercorns

2 bay leaves

1 carrot, halved

Posh Jambon Beurre dressing (makes enough for 6 sandwiches):

1 heaped tsp Dijon mustard

1 tbsp white wine vinegar

2 small round shallots, very finely chopped

20 small cornichons, roughly chopped into chunks (even just in half)

2 tbsp capers, rinsed and chopped

2 tbsp finely chopped tarragon

3 tbsp finely chopped flat-leaf parsley

4 tbsp good-quality olive oil

freshly ground black pepper, to taste

The Hawaiian pineapple chutney:

2 tbsp neutral oil

1 tsp black mustard seeds

1 star anise

1 tbsp chopped fresh root ginger

1 red chilli, deseeded and finely chopped

500g (1lb 2oz) red onions, sliced

350g (12oz) pineapple, diced into 1cm (½in) chunks

1 apple, peeled, cored and diced into 5mm (¼in) chunks

6 tbsp soft dark brown sugar

120ml (½ cup) cider vinegar

150ml (⅔ cup) water

salt, to taste

To serve:

crusty sourdough baguettes

salted butter (preferably French), cut in thick slabs

good Cheddar (such as Montgomery's), in slabs

THE HAM

1. Put the ham hocks in a large stock-pot or deep heavy saucepan and cover with water by 3cm (1in). Bring up to a simmer, then remove the hocks and discard the liquid. Place the hocks back in the clean pot with the rest of the ingredients and cover again with water. Bring to the boil, then reduce the heat to a very gentle simmer cook for about 3 hours, or until very soft and happily falling off the bone.

2. Remove from the heat and allow to cool for a while in the stock. Remove the hocks and roughly shred the meat, discarding the bones, skin and any gristly bits you don't fancy eating. This is your ham; you have made enough for lots of sandwiches. Strain the stock and add a little to the pulled ham if you plan to store it (it will keep in the refrigerator for up to 4 days). Use leftovers for a multitude of delicious things (it also freezes very well).

POSH JAMBON BEURRE

1. Combine all the dressing ingredients and set aside for 30 minutes or so.

2. Load the baguettes with butter, pulled ham and loads of dressing. Wrap 'em up and nip off to find your mates.

THE HAWAIIAN

1. For the pineapple chutney, heat the oil in a heavy saucepan over a medium-high heat and add the mustard seeds and star anise. When the mustard seeds crackle, add the ginger and chilli, shortly followed by the onions. Reduce the heat to medium and cook for about 30 minutes, stirring frequently, until the onions are dark, sweet and sticky.

2. Add the pineapple, apple and brown sugar and cook until any residual moisture has gone and everything is starting to caramelise. Pour in the vinegar and water and season lightly with a little salt. Reduce the heat to low and cook for about 1 hour, stirring occasionally, until dark, rich and glossy, topping up with a little water from time to time if necessary. Remove from the heat and leave to cool. Transfer to sterilised jars. It will keep for up to 2 months in the refrigerator.

3. To serve, butter the bread liberally, then load with your ham, chutney and Cheddar.

KOREAN SCOTCH EGGS

Spicy, garlicky and sweet. Dusting your eggs in a little flour once cooked prevents any gaps from forming as they fry.

SERVES 4–6

6 large eggs

100g (¾ cup) plain
(all-purpose) flour

1 tsp fine sea salt

80g (2 cups) panko breadcrumbs

2 tbsp white sesame seeds

1 tbsp black sesame seeds

2 eggs

2 tbsp milk

neutral oil, for deep-frying

Pork mix:

600g (1lb 5oz) fatty minced
(ground) pork

2 tbsp gochujang
(Korean hot pepper paste)

1 heaped tsp soft dark brown sugar

1 garlic clove, grated

1 heaped tsp grated fresh
root ginger

1 tsp gochugaru
(Korean red pepper flakes)

2 spring onions (scallions),
finely chopped

1½ tsp freshly ground black pepper

salt, to taste

1. Bring a large, shallow saucepan of water to a light simmer and carefully lower in your whole eggs. Cook for 6 minutes, then drain and rinse under running cold water for a few minutes to cool. Peel and set aside.

2. Combine the flour with the fine sea salt in a shallow bowl and set aside.

3. In a large bowl, mix the pork with the remaining coating ingredients and a good amount of salt until thoroughly combined. Divide the mixture into 6 equal portions. Evenly spread out a portion of meat on a piece of clingfilm (plastic wrap), then lightly dust a cooked egg in the seasoned flour and place it in the middle. Use the clingfilm to gather the meat evenly around the egg to enclose, then use your hands to shape into a even, smooth egg shape. Repeat the process with the other meat portions and eggs, then refrigerate for 30 minutes.

4. Meanwhile, mix the panko breadcrumbs with the two types of sesame seeds in a shallow bowl. Beat the eggs with the milk in a separate bowl. Using your dominant hand, roll a chilled meatball in the seasoned flour and shake a couple of times to remove any excess. Lower the ball into the egg mixture and, using your other hand, turn to coat evenly. Allow excess egg to drain back into the bowl, then transfer the ball to the sesame breadcrumbs and turn with your 'dry' hand until evenly coated. Set aside and repeat with the rest.

5. Heat the oil in a deep, heavy saucepan to 175°C (350°F). Working in batches, fry the Scotch eggs for about 5 minutes, or until the pork is cooked through and they are crisp and richly golden. If they are darkening too quickly, remove from the oil and transfer to a hot oven for a few minutes to finish cooking through. Drain on kitchen paper, then go to the park!

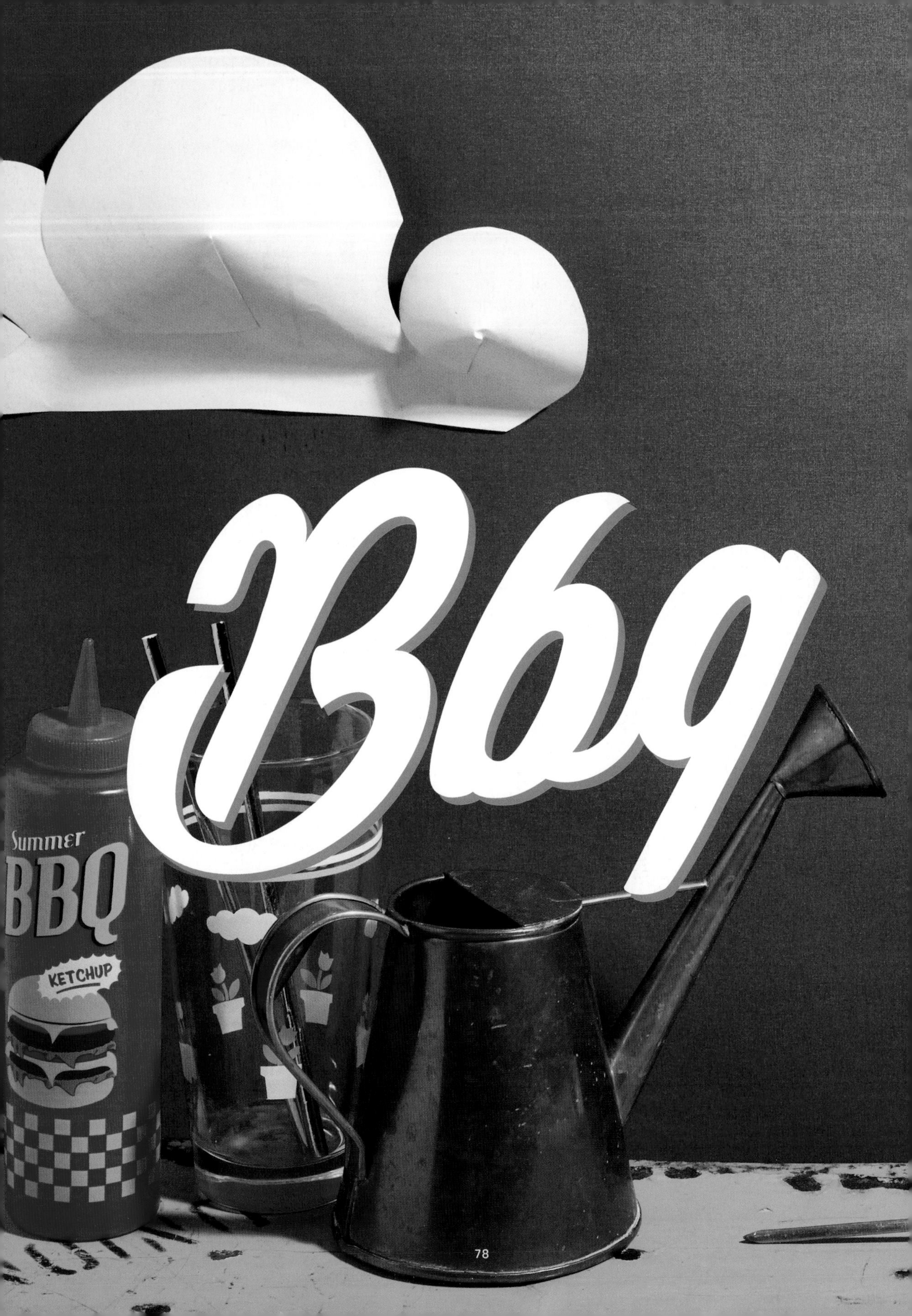
Bbq
Summer
BBQ
KETCHUP

Pit(bull)master

History must be full of unacknowledged, miserable chefs, but the turnspit dog is perhaps the most woeful of all. This poor creature, similar in size and shape to the modern corgi, was bred solely to run in a large fireside hamster wheel. This, with the help of various cogs and ropes, rotated large haunches of meat over medieval hearths. Often these animals worked in shifts, selflessly and tirelessly running their lives away to ensure even roasting for the table. The last known example of a turnspit dog, Whisky, has earned his eternal rest and now sits proudly in a glass case at the Abergavenny Museum, Wales.

CHEESY GARLIC BAGUETTES WITH SPICY HONEY

81

GRILLED STREET CORN NACHOS

82

JALAPEÑO POPPER BACON SLAW

84

GRILLED LOADED POTATO SKINS SALAD

85

GLAZED BBQ SAUSAGE KEBABS

87

GRILLED PINEAPPLE HOT SAUCE MARGARITAS

87

ALABAMA BBQ CHICKEN

88

BUFFALO BBQ RIBS

91

GRILLED NECTARINE PANZANELLA WITH BURRATA

92

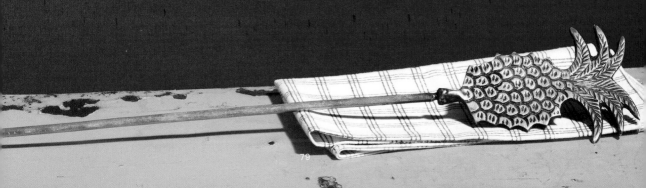

CHEESY GARLIC BAGUETTES WITH SPICY HONEY

You can use any cheeses you like for this. The Roquefort is delicious with the spicy honey, but you can leave it out if you don't like blue cheese and bulk the mixture out with another one of your favourites, such as Parmesan, if you like.

SERVES 6

Spicy honey:

2 mild red chillies, sliced

250g (scant 1 cup) honey

Breads:

100g (1½ cups) Parmesan, grated

125g (1 cup) Comté or Gruyère cheese, grated

50g (2oz) Roquefort, crumbled (optional)

3 tbsp finely chopped chives

2 tbsp finely chopped flat-leaf parsley

125g unsalted butter, softened

50g (scant ¼ cup) mayonnaise

4 fat garlic cloves, grated

2 crusty French baguettes

salt and freshly ground black pepper, to taste

1. For the spicy honey, combine the chillies and honey in a small saucepan and set over the very lowest heat. Allow the mixture to infuse and reduce, stirring occasionally, for about 1 hour, then remove from the heat and leave to cool.

2. For the baguettes, preheat your barbecue and prepare for indirect grilling (shove most of the hot coals over to one side).

3. In a large bowl, beat together the cheeses, herbs, butter, mayonnaise and garlic until well combined. Season well with salt and pepper.

4. Slice the baguettes on an angle along their length – almost to the base, but not all the way through. Using a fork or spoon, divide the cheese mixture between the breads, pushing it down between the cracks until they are all well stuffed.

5. Wrap the baguettes in a couple of layers of foil, gathering it up around the sides but leaving the tops exposed. Place the baguettes on the cooler side of the barbecue grill and close the lid (if it has one). Grill for 15–20 minutes, or until the baguettes are crisp, melting and smoky.

6. Take to the table and drizzle spicy honey over the top.

GRILLED STREET CORN NACHOS

Elotes is a hugely popular Mexican street food, and is really delicious. Husks of corn are grilled street-side, slathered with mayonnaise-laced crema, topped with cotija cheese and chilli and served with wedges of lime. These nachos take inspiration from the posher, off-the-cob version, called *esquites* (like a creamy Mexican corn salad), and are unashamedly inauthentic, but very good. Leave out the beef chilli for a veggie version.

SERVES 6

1 bunch of spring onions (scallions)

3 jalapeño chillies

4 corn cobs

a drizzle of olive oil

400g (14oz) corn tortilla chips

400g (1⅔ cups) leftover beef chilli (optional)

300g (3 cups) Cheddar, grated

1 small red onion, finely chopped

juice of ½ lime

½ tsp cumin seeds, toasted and ground

50g (2oz) feta cheese, crumbled

Turkish pepper flakes (pul biber), to taste

a handful of fresh coriander (cilantro), finely chopped

salt, to taste

Dressing:

1 lime

100g (scant ½ cup) mayonnaise

200g (1 cup) sour cream

½ garlic clove, grated

salt, to taste

1. Preheat your barbecue or a grill (broiler) to high.

2. Rub the spring onions, jalapeños and corn cobs with a little oil and season with salt. Grill (broil), turning frequently, until softened and charred in places.

3. Slice the kernels from the grilled corn cobs and roughly chop the spring onions and chillies.

4. Put half of the corn kernels into a blender and process to a purée, loosening with a little water and olive oil to help it along. Season with salt and set aside.

5. Zest the whole lime (reserving the zest for later), then cut it in half and place, flesh-side down, on the hot barbecue grill until pleasingly charred. Set aside.

6. Grab some foil trays (or fashion a large tray with a double layer of strong foil) and poke some holes in the base. Spread half of the tortilla chips over the bottom of the tray/s and top with half of the beef chilli (if using), half of the grated Cheddar, half of the remaining corn kernels and half of the chopped grilled chillies and spring onions. Repeat with the other half of the ingredients. Place on the cooler side of your barbecue, close the lid (if it has one) and cook for about 10 minutes.

7. Meanwhile, make the dressing. In a small bowl, mix together the mayonnaise, sour cream and garlic along with the reserved lime zest. Squeeze in the juice from the grilled lime. Season lightly with salt and set aside.

8. In a separate small bowl, dress the red onion with the lime juice and the toasted ground cumin.

9. By now, the nachos should be hot through, smoky and oozy, and perhaps a little charred in places. Plonk them, foil and all, in the middle of the table, and liberally sloosh over the sour cream dressing and dot around the corn purée. Put any leftover dressing and purée in bowls on the table for dipping. Cover the lot with crumbled feta, Turkish pepper flakes, plenty of coriander and the zingy onions. Dig in.

JALAPEÑO POPPER BACON SLAW

 p.83

Although coleslaw is derived from the Dutch word *koolsla*, which means 'cabbage salad', in our eyes it is so much more than that. If it ain't creamy, it ain't slaw.

SERVES 4

1 medium white cabbage, finely sliced or finely shredded

2 tbsp sugar

1 tsp fine sea salt

2 large fresh jalapeño chillies

12 bacon rashers

50g (2oz) pickled jalapeños, drained and roughly chopped

3 celery sticks, sliced

1 medium white onion, finely sliced

1 small bunch of flat-leaf parsley, leaves only

Dressing:

150g (⅔ cup) cream cheese

100g (scant ½ cup) mayonnaise

2 tbsp white wine vinegar

juice of 1 lemon

2 tsp sugar

salt and freshly ground black pepper, to taste

1. Preheat the grill (broiler) to high.

2. Toss the cabbage in a bowl with the sugar and salt, then transfer to a colander set over a bowl and let stand for 1 hour.

3. Meanwhile, grill the whole jalapeño chillies until charred all over. Let cool, then deseed and slice into thin strips. Place in a large bowl and set aside.

4. Fry the bacon slices in a dry frying pan (skillet) over a medium heat until crispy, then remove, roughly chop and add to the bowl with the chillies.

5. Squeeze any remaining juices out of the cabbage and add to the bowl, along with the chopped pickled jalapeños, celery, onion and parsley.

6. Whisk together all the dressing ingredients until smooth, then toss through the salad until thoroughly mixed in. Serve.

GRILLED LOADED POTATO SKINS SALAD

 p.86

The humble potato and some storecupboard ingredients bulk out this thrifty yet deeply satisfying 'salad'. Proof that sides – done well – can be just as, if not more, exciting than mains.

SERVES 4

1.5kg (3lb 4oz) large baking potatoes, scrubbed

8 spring onions (scallions)

50ml (3½ tbsp) olive oil

salt and freshly ground black pepper, to taste

Dressing:

80ml (⅓ cup) sour cream

70g (⅓ cup) mayonnaise

2 tsp white wine vinegar

1 tbsp olive oil

1 tsp sugar

salt and freshly ground black pepper, to taste

To serve:

10 bacon rashers, sliced

50g (1 cup) chives, chopped

125g (1¼ cups) Double Gloucester cheese, finely grated

1. Prick the potatoes all over with a fork. Microwave them on high for 15–20 minutes, turning them halfway through. Alternatively, bake the potatoes in an oven preheated to 200°C/400°F/gas 6 until easily pierced with a knife.

2. Meanwhile, preheat your barbecue or grill (broiler) to high.

3. When cool enough to handle, halve the potatoes and scoop out the flesh with a spoon, leaving a 5mm (¼in) thick layer of potato on the inside of each skin. Cut the skin into wedges, then place in a bowl along with the whole spring onions and toss gently with oil and season with salt and pepper.

4. Grill (or broil) the potato skins and spring onions until they have good colour all over and are a little charred in places. Remove from the heat, then roughly chop the spring onions and place in a large bowl with the grilled wedges.

5. Fry the bacon slices in a dry frying pan (skillet) over a medium heat until crispy, then remove and set aside.

6. In a separate bowl, whisk together the sour cream, mayonnaise, vinegar, olive oil, sugar and salt and pepper to taste. Pour over the grilled veg in the bowl and gently toss together to coat.

7. Arrange the dressed potato skins and onions on a serving platter. Load with the crispy bacon, chives and grated cheese.

GLAZED BBQ SAUSAGE KEBABS

All those who've experienced British alfresco dining will recall sad burgers, rain and disappointment. However, despite the drizzle and occasionally rubbish food, we steadfastly retain a love for that barbecue staple: slightly burnt but shockingly juicy sausages cooked over charcoal, served in a crap floury bap with lashings of ketchup. This recipe attempts to bottle that memory and refine it, with bangers glazed in a very British homemade barbecue sauce.

SERVES 6

1 tbsp vegetable oil

1 medium onion, grated

1 garlic clove, crushed

1 large cooking apple, peeled and cut into chunks

200ml (scant 1 cup) ruby port

300ml (1¼ cups) apple juice

4 large rosemary sprigs, charred slightly over a flame, plus an extra sprig for brushing

200ml (scant 1 cup) cider vinegar

250g (generous 1 cup) ketchup

1 tbsp English mustard

150g (¾ cup) soft dark brown sugar

½ tsp cayenne pepper

12 good-quality sausages

salt and freshly ground black pepper, to taste

crusty baguettes, to serve

1. Preheat your barbecue until the flames have subsided and the coals have turned white.

2. Meanwhile, heat the oil in a medium saucepan over a low-medium heat and gently fry the onion and garlic until soft and sweet, about 10 minutes. Add the apple chunks and cook until tender to the point of a knife, about 10 minutes. Add the port, apple juice and rosemary sprigs, increase the heat and cook until reduced by half, about 10 minutes. Add the vinegar, ketchup, mustard, brown sugar and cayenne pepper, season with salt and pepper and continue to reduce for a further 10 minutes until thick.

3. Remove the pan from the heat and discard the rosemary. Pour the mixture into a blender and process until really smooth. If necessary, return to the pan to reduce the sauce further.

4. Skewer the sausages (up to 6 depending on the size of your grill) in rows on 2 parallel kebab sticks (this stops them spinning around when you flip them).

5. Grill the sausages over the hot coals until cooked through and crispy-skinned, about 5–10 minutes depending on the sausages.

6. When the sausages are nearly cooked, use a rosemary sprig dipped in the sauce to baste them all over and continue to cook over the flames until they are sticky and delicious looking.

7. Serve in baguettes, drizzled with more of the sauce.

 Grilled pineapple hot sauce margaritas

We like to serve this one in a pineapple fruit bowl, because – well – it's more fun. To do this, chop the head off a pineapple and neatly scoop out the innards, retaining them for grilling. No dramas.

SERVES 3–4

12–15 chopped pineapple chunks

2 tbsp unsalted butter, melted

2 tbsp caster (superfine) sugar

150ml (⅔ cup) silver tequila

60ml (¼ cup) triple sec

150ml (⅔ cup) pineapple juice

75ml (⅓ cup) lime juice

20 (ish) drops of Tabasco sauce

25ml (1½ tbsp) sugar syrup (or agave syrup)

3 large scoops ice (crushed works best)

1. Preheat the barbecue or grill (broiler) to high.

2. Brush the pineapple chunks with the melted butter and sprinkle with the sugar. Transfer to the barbecue or grill and grill (or broil) until golden brown and caramelised. Remove as and when the pieces are ready, then chill them in the refrigerator.

3. Add the pineapple chunks (reserving a few pieces for garnish) along with the remaining ingredients to a blender or food processor and blend to a slushy consistency.

4. Pour into glasses and garnish with the reserved grilled pineapple, umbrellas and straws.

ALABAMA BBQ CHICKEN

Invented by Robert 'Big Bob' Gibson at his restaurant down in Decatur, (wait for it) Alabama, white barbecue sauce is a legit alternative to the traditional ketchup/molasses versions, and is really easy to make. Down at Big Bob's they 'baptise' whole hickory-smoked chickens in the stuff, as part of an offering that has won them over fifteen World Barbecue Championships. If it's good enough for Bob! This is our version, zesty with lemon and hot with fresh horseradish and black pepper.

SERVES 4–6

1 tbsp paprika

½ tsp smoked paprika

1 tsp freshly ground black pepper

1 tbsp cumin seeds, coarsely ground

2 tsp salt

6 chicken legs, at room temperature

1 tbsp olive oil, plus extra as needed

2–3 spring onions (scallions), sliced, to serve

4 tbsp finely chopped chives, to serve

pul biber (Turkish pepper flakes) or cayenne pepper, to serve (optional)

Alabama Sauce:

250g (generous 1 cup) mayonnaise

75g (2½oz) fresh horseradish, peeled and finely grated

100ml (generous ⅓ cup) good-quality cider vinegar

75ml (⅓ cup) cloudy apple juice

1 heaped tsp American (yellow) mustard

1 garlic clove, crushed to a paste

1 tbsp brown sugar

zest of 1 unwaxed lemon

½ tsp celery salt

1 heaped tsp freshly ground black pepper

salt, to taste

1. Preheat the oven to 180°C/350°F/gas 4. Line a baking tray with greaseproof paper.

2. Combine the paprikas, black pepper, ground cumin and salt and rub the mixture all over the chicken legs. Pat them all with the olive oil, then place on the prepared baking tray. Roast for 1 hour, or until the meat easily pulls away from the bone at the drum end.

3. Meanwhile, preheat your barbecue for direct grilling.

4. Combine the sauce ingredients. Don't worry if it looks a little thin – this is how it should be! It should taste tangy, fragrant, a little sweet, and hot with black pepper and horseradish.

5. When the barbecue is hot, transfer the cooked chicken legs to the grill (drizzling over a little more olive oil beforehand if they look as though they need it) and cook on both sides until crisp and a little charred, about 5 minutes. Keep them moving to avoid flare-ups or burning. When they look about ready, baste them liberally with the Alabama sauce, flip and repeat. Do this 2 or 3 times before removing from the grill to a serving plate to rest for a few minutes.

6. To serve, lacquer over more of the fresh sauce and adorn with the spring onions and chives. Flick over the pul biber (Turkish pepper flakes) or cayenne pepper (if using). Transfer the rest of the sauce to a bowl ready for dunking. Great with cornbread.

BUFFALO BBQ RIBS

TGI Fridays, the original Americana powerhouse, do a stellar rack of baby backs. Their barbecue sauce was always a bit spicy, not unlike this one. You can take these ribs any which way you like, but this oven-then-grill method of cooking is a winner. Make sure to buy good-quality, fatty ribs.

SERVES 4

2 x 1kg (2lb 3oz) racks baby back pork ribs

1 tbsp garlic powder

1 tbsp smoked paprika

1½ tbsp paprika

3 tbsp brown sugar

1½ tsp fennel seeds, coarsely ground

1½ tbsp fine sea salt

2 tbsp coarsely ground black pepper

75g (⅓ cup) unsalted butter

250ml (generous 1 cup) barbecue sauce

250ml (generous 1 cup) hot sauce (we like Frank's)

2 tbsp honey

1. Preheat the oven to 150°C/300°F/gas 2.

2. Remove the silverskin or membrane from the underside of the rib racks and pat dry with kitchen paper.

3. Combine the garlic powder, paprikas, brown sugar, ground fennel seeds, salt and black pepper in a bowl, then liberally cover the rib racks with the mixture.

4. Pop both racks into a large roasting pan and cover tightly with foil. Roast in the oven for 2 hours until the ribs are soft but still (just) holding their shape, then remove from the oven.

5. Melt the butter in a small saucepan, then add the barbecue sauce, hot sauce and honey and heat through. Blend with a hand-held stick (immersion) blender until emulsified and lighter in colour.

6. Preheat your barbecue or grill (broiler) to high.

7. Baste the ribs liberally with the sauce and place on (or under) the hot grill. Grill (or broil) for 2 minutes, then flip and baste the other side. Repeat this a couple of times, until the glaze has caramelised and the ribs tear away with ease.

8. Transfer the racks to a board, separate into ribs and serve!

GRILLED NECTARINE PANZANELLA WITH BURRATA

Burrata completes this classic panzanella bread salad recipe, in the way that only a massive, cream-filled ball of cheese can. Absolutely perfect for a summer's day dreaming of Tuscany – panzanella's spiritual home.

SERVES 3–4

2 large red peppers

2 large yellow peppers

4 nectarines, pitted and cut into thick slices

4½ tbsp olive oil

400g (14oz) firm, good-quality, day-old bread, sliced

2 tbsp, plus 1 tsp red wine vinegar

1 red onion, thinly sliced

1 tbsp caster (superfine) sugar

juice of 1 lemon

1 garlic clove, crushed

500g (1lb 2oz) ripe mixed tomatoes, cut into wedges

a large handful of basil, roughly torn

salt and freshly ground black pepper, to taste

3 burrata, to serve

1. Preheat your barbecue until the flames have subsided and the coals have turned white.

2. Grill the peppers in their skins until completely blackened all over, then transfer to a bowl and cover with clingfilm (plastic wrap) to steam for a few minutes. When cool enough to handle, peel off the blackened skins, slice the peppers into thick slivers and set aside.

3. In a bowl, toss the nectarine slices in 1½ tbsp of the olive oil, until well coated. Grill the slices until they are a little charred, then set aside.

4. Using your fingers, sprinkle the bread slices with 2 tbsp of the red wine vinegar, then toast on the grill and set aside.

5. In a large bowl, mix the red onion with the sugar and lemon juice and leave to macerate for around 20 minutes.

6. Add the remaining 1 tsp of red wine vinegar, the remaining 3 tbsp of olive oil and the garlic to the onions, then add the sliced, cooked peppers, the tomatoes with their juices, the grilled nectarine slices and the basil. Tear the toasted bread into rough chunks and add to the mix, then toss to combine. Season to taste.

7. Transfer the salad to a large platter then tear over the burrata, drizzling with a little more olive oil if you like.

Fast Fuel

Given all that we know about the fast food industry, you'd think that the world's top sportsmen and women would do well to steer clear. As it turns out, a shocking number of elite performers have relied almost exclusively upon fast food giants to propel them to success. In 2008, Usain Bolt charged to Olympic glory, fuelled by a daily diet of over one hundred Chicken McNuggets from a Beijing McDonald's. This was supplemented by dozens of cartons of French fries and the occasional apple pie. At the same Games, swimmer Ryan Lochte won four medals by eating at the Golden Arches for breakfast, lunch and dinner, while legendary NFL wide- receiver Chad Johnson has allegedly spent his entire life a dedicated disciple of the McDonald's diet.

SICILIAN MEATBALL SANDWICHES

A little sweet, very garlicky and hot from the black pepper, these really are the most delicious meatballs. The cold cheese and the soaked bread panade keep these good and tender, but it's important not to overwork the mix. We also like to keep them quite large and grill (broil) them, as frying meatballs can dry them out. If you don't fancy sandwiches, these are also amazing with pasta.

SERVES 4–6

Sauce:

2 tbsp olive oil

2 garlic cloves, thinly sliced

150ml (⅔ cup) red wine

3 x 400g (14oz) cans top-quality plum tomatoes, crushed

100g (scant ½ cup) unsalted butter

1 medium onion, halved

1 tsp white sugar

salt, to taste

Meatballs:

4 slices of white bread (preferably stale), crusts removed

1 large onion

500g (1lb 2oz) minced (ground) beef

500g (1lb 2oz) minced (ground) pork

1½ tbsp flaked sea salt

1½ tbsp ground black pepper

2 tsp whole fennel seeds, coarsely ground

1 large egg, plus 1 large egg yolk

6 garlic cloves, crushed to a paste

40g (generous ¼ cup) pine nuts, toasted

60g (scant ½ cup) raisins, coarsely chopped

60g (1 cup) fridge-cold Parmesan, grated

a handful of fresh oregano or marjoram, leaves only, finely chopped

To serve:

crusty French baguettes or hoagie-style rolls

salted butter

fresh rocket (arugula)

grated Parmesan

1. For the sauce, heat the olive oil in a saucepan over a medium heat, add the garlic and fry until just starting to colour. Add the red wine and reduce over a high heat until almost completely evaporated, then add all of the other sauce ingredients. Bring to a simmer, then reduce the heat to low and cook for about 1 hour until the fat separates and it tastes good. Adjust the seasoning if necessary.

2. Meanwhile, make the meatballs. Tear or chop your bread into small pieces and place in the bottom of a large, wide bowl. Coarsely grate over the onion and mix well to combine. There should be just enough moisture from the onion to hydrate the bread; if not, add 1 tsp or so of water. Leave to rest for 10 minutes, then add one-third of each of the meats, the salt, black pepper, ground fennel seeds, whole egg and egg yolk, and the garlic. Mix thoroughly until everything is evenly distributed – it should be pasty and wet. Add the rest of the meat along with the pine nuts, chopped raisins, Parmesan and fresh herbs. Mix until everything is the same colour and it has just come together, but try not to overwork.

3. Preheat the grill (broiler) to high and line a baking tray with greaseproof paper.

4. Form the mixture into 12–14 large meatballs and place on the prepared tray, then slide under the grill (aim for 5cm/2in from the element). Grill (broil) for 6–8 minutes on each side, or until you have achieved a good colour all over (don't worry if some of the pine nuts singe a little). At this point your meatballs should be almost cooked through.

5. Drop the meatballs into the pan with the tomato sauce and simmer gently for a few minutes or so over a low heat, to finish cooking them through. You can test one for doneness – although they are forgiving, cooking them for too long in the sauce will result in tough meatballs.

6. If the meatballs are destined for a sandwich, butter the bread liberally, then stuff with meatballs, rocket, a little extra sauce and lashings of Parmesan.

HUNTER'S CHICKEN MOZZARELLA STICKS

In the UK, Hunter's Chicken involves barbecue sauce, bacon, Cheddar and (unsurprisingly) chicken. Confusingly, France and Italy also have their own versions of Hunter's Chicken, neither of which have anything to do with ours, which is inspired by the BBQ Chicken Melt you used to be able to get at Wetherspoons pubs.

SERVES 4

3 chicken breasts,
cooked and shredded

250ml (generous 1 cup)
barbecue sauce

150g (5½oz) streaky bacon, chopped

100g (generous 1 cup)
mature Cheddar, grated

100g (scant 1 cup)
mozzarella, grated

100g (¾ cup) plain
(all-purpose) flour

1 tsp cayenne pepper

1 tsp garlic powder

3 eggs, beaten with a little milk

120g (2 cups) fine breadcrumbs

neutral oil, for deep-frying

salt and freshly ground
black pepper

1. Mix the shredded chicken with the barbecue sauce.

2. Fry the bacon in a dry frying pan (skillet) until crisp, then drain off the fat. Allow the bacon to cool a little, then add to the BBQ chicken mix. Add the cheeses and mix together, then season with salt and pepper to taste. Press the mixture into a loaf pan lined with clingfilm (plastic wrap). Cover the top with clingfilm and place in the freezer for 2 hours to set until solid.

3. When frozen, remove from the freezer and let thaw a little, then unwrap. Cut the block into about 12 fish finger-sized sticks.

4. Put the flour into a shallow wide bowl and season with the cayenne pepper, garlic powder and 1 tsp salt. Place the beaten eggs in a separate bowl and put the breadcrumbs into another bowl.

5. Dip the sticks one at a time into the flour, shaking off any excess, then into the egg mix, allowing any excess to drip back into the bowl, and finally into the breadcrumbs, gently rolling them around to get a good coating.

6. Heat the oil in a deep, heavy saucepan to 180ºC (350ºF). Fry the coated sticks in batches until crisp, 3–4 minutes. Remove with a slotted spoon and briefly drain on kitchen paper.

TERIYAKI BEEF BUNS

p.99

Dark and heady with the exotic aroma of Chinese five-spice, these slow-cooked glazed beef buns are the perfect thing to chow down on with your sport-adoring pals. Originally a method of cooking from Japan, our teriyaki leans more towards the Americanised variation popular worldwide today.

SERVES 6

Beef buns:

3 tbsp groundnut oil

1.2kg (2lb 12 oz) braising steak, cut into 4cm (1½in) chunks

1 tbsp sesame seeds

3 garlic cloves, crushed

50g (1¾oz) fresh root ginger, finely diced

1½ tbsp Chinese five-spice

salt, to taste

500ml (generous 2 cups) beef stock

1 tbsp dark soy sauce

1 tbsp light soy sauce

1 tbsp sesame oil

2½ tbsp caster (superfine) sugar

2 tbsp cornflour (cornstarch)

1 tsp water

8 soft buns

Slaw:

¼ red cabbage, finely shredded (use a mandoline if you have one)

1 large carrot, finely shredded

1 apple, unpeeled, finely shredded

4 spring onions (scallions), thinly sliced on the diagonal

1 medium red chilli, deseeded and sliced

170g (¾ cup) mayonnaise

juice of 1½ limes

½ tsp salt

a large handful of coriander (cilantro), chopped

1. Heat 2 tbsp of the oil in a large heavy sauté pan (preferably with a lid) over a high heat and quickly sear the beef, until coloured all over. You will need to do this in batches. Remove from the pan and set aside in a bowl.

2. Add the remaining oil then turn the temperature down to low. Fry the sesame seeds until just turning golden, then add the garlic and ginger and fry for 30 seconds until fragrant.

3. Return the beef to the pan, stir through the Chinese five-spice and salt, pour over the stock and bring to barely a simmer. Cook gently for about 3 hours, until soft. Top up with water if the pan looks dry and stir every now and then.

4. When ready, bring back to a simmer and add the soy sauces, sesame oil and sugar. In a small bowl, mix the cornflour and water together and add this to the sauce, then stir to thicken it all together at a gentle simmer.

5. Meanwhile, mix together all of the slaw ingredients in a large bowl and set aside.

6. Toast the buns and fill each with the teriyaki beef, then the slaw. Serve warm.

CHEESEBURGER-STUFFED DOUGH BALLS

 p.102

The original provenance of the burger is difficult to pinpoint; some say they come from Hamburg in Germany, others that they hail from the good old US of A. Whoever came up with the idea first, we can gladly leave open to debate. The point is, the burger is here to stay – from the glorious to the terrible, ground meat in a bun has taken over the world. Our slant is wrapping the flavours of the cheeseburger in some of the softest dough you've ever tried, making them the perfect pre-match appetiser.

SERVES 6

1 x quantity Milk Buns recipe **(p.22)**

2 tsp vegetable oil

8 thick-cut streaky bacon rashers, finely chopped

450g (1lb) minced (ground) beef

2 garlic cloves, crushed

1 tbsp plain (all-purpose) flour

500ml (generous 2 cups) beef stock

24 x 1cm (½in) cubes of Double Gloucester/Cheddar cheese

1 egg

2 tsp milk

½ tsp salt

sesame seeds, for sprinkling

burger sauce, to serve

salt and freshly ground black pepper, to taste

1. First make your milk bread dough according to steps 1–4 of the recipe on **p.22** (it will need at least 1 hour to rise).

2. Heat the oil in a saucepan over a medium heat, add the bacon and fry until crispy, about 5 minutes. Increase the heat and add the beef, breaking it apart with a wooden spoon. Cook for about 10 minutes until well browned and starting to crisp in places. Reduce the heat a little, then stir through the garlic and cook until aromatic, about 1 minute. Sprinkle in the flour and stir to coat the meat, then cook for about 2 minutes until the flour is golden brown.

3. Add the beef stock and season well. Bring to a gentle simmer and cook, stirring every so often, until the mixture is reduced and thick, about 20 minutes. Remove from the heat and let cool completely.

4. Divide the milk bread dough into 24 pieces (each about 30g/1oz) and shape into balls. Keep the dough covered with a cloth while working with each dough ball, so it doesn't dry out.

5. Press each dough ball flat into a disc, about 2cm (¾in) thick. Place 1 tbsp of the beef mixture in the middle of each disc, then press 1 cube of cheese inside. Wrap the bread dough around the filling, from the edges inwards, and pinch in the middle to seal.

6. Line a baking tray with greaseproof paper, then arrange each filled bun on the tray, with a little bit of space in between each one. Cover with a cloth or clingfilm (plastic wrap) and set aside for about 30 minutes to rise until doubled in size.

7. Meanwhile, preheat the oven to 180°C/350°F/gas 4.

8. Whisk together the egg, milk and salt. Brush each bun gently and evenly with the egg wash and then sprinkle with sesame seeds.

9. Bake the buns for 15–18 minutes until golden brown, rotating the tray halfway through cooking.

10. Serve with your favourite burger sauce and enjoy!

MINI TACOS 3 WAYS

If tiny little tacos doesn't scream 'I'm watching sport', then what does? You'll never look at a muffin pan in the same way.

SERVES 4–6

For the Mini Pizza Tacos:

6–7 x 25cm (10in) tortillas

125g (generous ½ cup) unsalted butter, melted

1 tsp garlic powder

1 tsp dried oregano

225g (1 cup) ready-made pizza sauce

170g (1½ cups) mozzarella, grated

about 50 pepperoni slices

For the Mini Chicken Fajita Tacos:

6–7 x 25cm (10in) tortillas

125g (generous ½ cup) unsalted butter, melted

3 tbsp fajita seasoning

2 tsp vegetable oil

1 onion, finely diced

½ each red, green and yellow peppers, finely diced

250g (1½ cups) cooked, shredded chicken

225g (1 cup) cream cheese

140g (1½ cups) Cheddar, grated

chopped flat-leaf parsley, for sprinkling

For the Mini Buffalo Chicken Tacos:

6–7 x 25cm (10in) tortillas

125g (generous ½ cup) unsalted butter, melted

100ml (generous ⅓ cup) hot sauce (we like Frank's)

½ tsp garlic powder

½ tsp smoked paprika

250g (1½ cups) cooked, shredded chicken

125g (generous ½ cup) cream cheese

1 spring onion (scallion), finely chopped

½ tsp fine sea salt

90g (¾ cup) mozzarella, grated

2 tbsp finely chopped chives

1. Preheat the oven to 200°C/400°F/gas 6.
2. Cut 4–5 rounds out of each tortilla with a 7.5cm (3in) cookie cutter to get about 25–30 rounds.

MINI PIZZA TACOS

1. In a bowl, mix together the butter, garlic powder and oregano.
2. Toss each tortilla round in the butter mixture to coat.
3. Flip a muffin or cupcake pan upside down and tuck the tortilla rounds in between the cups to give them a curved shape. Bake for 6–7 minutes until just golden brown. Remove from the oven and let cool.
4. Fill each taco shell with a spoonful of pizza sauce and top with grated mozzarella and pepperoni slices. Arrange on a baking tray and bake for 5–6 minutes until the cheese has melted.

MINI CHICKEN FAJITA TACOS

1. In a bowl, mix together the butter and half of the fajita seasoning..
2. Toss each tortilla round in the butter mixture to coat.
3. Flip a muffin or cupcake pan upside down and tuck the tortilla rounds in between the cups to give them a curved shape. Bake for 6–7 minutes until just golden brown. Remove from the oven and let cool.
4. Heat the oil in a saucepan over a medium heat, add the onion and peppers and cook, stirring constantly, for about 10–15 minutes, until they are soft and caramelised. Remove from the heat and let cool.
5. In a large bowl, mix the shredded chicken with the cooked peppers and onion, the remaining fajita spice, cream cheese and three-quarters of the cheese.
6. Fill each taco with a spoonful of the chicken mixture and top with the remaining cheese. Arrange on a baking tray and bake for 5–6 minutes until the cheese has melted. Sprinkle with chopped parsley.

MINI BUFFALO CHICKEN TACOS

1. In a bowl, mix together the butter with 3 tbsp of the hot sauce, the garlic powder and smoked paprika.
2. Toss each tortilla round in the butter mixture to coat.
3. Flip a muffin or cupcake pan upside down and tuck the tortilla rounds in between the cups to give them a curved shape. Bake for 6–7 minutes until just golden brown. Remove from the oven and let cool.
4. Meanwhile, combine the chicken, cream cheese, spring onion, salt and the remaining hot sauce in a bowl.
5. Fill each taco with a teaspoonful of the chicken mixture and top with a pinch of mozzarella. Arrange on a baking tray and bake for 5 minutes until the cheese has just melted. Top with chives and dig in!

FIVE-SPICE PULLED PORK

The best homemade Chinese five-spice blends often contain more than five spices (go figure). Whichever you go for, it's important to have a blend of liquorice-scented spices – especially for this recipe, as it really is amazing with pork. Make sure to find good Sichuan peppercorns; some supermarket varieties taste oddly like cheap potpourri. As ever, if you're investing lots of time into cooking a recipe, invest in your meat, too. You want the fat from a happy pig.

SERVES 6

1 tbsp Sichuan peppercorns

2 tsp black peppercorns

5cm (2in) piece of cinnamon stick, broken into pieces

2 tbsp fennel seeds

2 star anise, broken into pieces

2 tsp anise seeds (optional)

1½ tbsp fine sea salt

2 tbsp soft dark brown sugar

1 tsp ground ginger

1 x 2–2.5kg (4lb 6oz–5lb 8oz) neck end, bone-in pork shoulder joint, skin and some fat removed

To serve:

buns, split and toasted

fresh herbs, sauces, pickles or slaw (you choose)

1. Preheat the oven to 220°C/425°F/gas 7.

2. Toast the Sichuan peppercorns, black peppercorns, cinnamon stick, fennel seeds and star anise in a dry cast-iron (or heavy) pan until starting to smoke. Cool, then combine with the anise seeds (if using) in a pestle and mortar or spice grinder. Grind to a coarse powder, then mix in the salt, sugar and ground ginger. Massage the spice mixture all over the pork joint.

3. Place the joint, fat-side up, on a rack in a large roasting pan and roast for 25–30 minutes, or until it has taken on a good colour all over (do not let it burn). Remove from the oven, turn the heat down to 120°C/250°F/gas ½ and wait for it to come to temperature. Cover the tray with foil, leaving room for the steam to circulate, place the pork back in the oven and cook until the meat is happily falling away from the bone. This should take about 6 hours, but start checking after 5 hours. The internal temperature of the joint should hit 90°C/194°F on a meat thermometer when it's ready.

4. Remove from the oven, discard the foil and turn the heat up to 230°C/450°F/gas 8. Pop the pork back in the oven for 10 minutes or so to get it nice and crisp.

5. Rest the pork for 30 minutes out of the oven, covered, then pull into rough, bite-size chunks (don't overwork it, or it will be mushy and not as nice to eat). Dress with any juices from the cooking and/or resting.

6. Load into toasted buns and adorn with garnishes of your choosing.

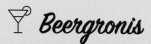 **Beergronis** p.102

This makes one drink, but we do encourage you to make more. Unless you're watching the game on your own? In which case, at least two.

MAKES 1

25ml (1½ tbsp) gin

25ml (1½ tbsp) sweet vermouth

25ml (1½ tbsp) Campari

25ml (1½ tbsp) orange juice

ice cubes

about 100ml (generous ⅓ cup) American-style IPA beer (such as Punk IPA)

1–2 orange slices, to serve

1. Add the gin, sweet vermouth, Campari and orange juice to a cocktail shaker along with a scoop of ice cubes and shake hard for at least 10 seconds.

2. Using a cocktail strainer as well as a fine strainer (or sieve), double strain the cocktail into a short glass over some fresh ice cubes.

3. Top up the glass to the rim with the beer and garnish with a slice or two of orange.

DOUGH BALL DIP TRAY

As party starters go, whipping a batch of these out is second only to owning a swimming pool or a brewery. Great if some of your pals are veggie.

....

SERVES 4–6

1 x Milk Buns recipe **(p.22)**

1 egg

½ tsp fine sea salt

1 tsp water

Buffalo Chicken Dip:

225g (1 cup) cream cheese, softened

500g (3 cups) cooked, shredded chicken

115g (scant ½ cup) hot sauce

115g (½ cup) sour cream

1 garlic clove, minced

1 tbsp chopped chives

70g (¾ cup) Double Gloucester cheese, grated, for topping

salt and freshly ground black pepper, to taste

Spinach and Artichoke Dip:

225g (1 cup) cream cheese, softened

125g (generous ½ cup) mayonnaise

125g (generous ½ cup) sour cream

30g (½ cup) grated Parmesan

125g (4½oz) canned artichokes, chopped

125g (4½oz) frozen spinach, thawed, drained and chopped

1 garlic clove, minced

225g (2 cups) mozzarella, grated, for topping

salt and freshly ground black pepper, to taste

1. First make your milk bread dough according to steps 1–4 of the recipe on **p.22** (it will need at least 1 hour to rise).

2. Grease and line a 33 x 43cm (13 x 17in) deep baking tray (sheet pan).

3. In separate bowls, mix together all the ingredients for each dip, leaving out the final quantity of cheese for each. Make sure each is well combined and season to taste.

4. Divide and roll the milk bread dough into golf balls and place around the edge of the tray and across the middle to create two rectangles.

5. Tip one dip mixture into each half and smooth over the surface.

6. Top the buffalo chicken dip with the Double Gloucester cheese and top the spinach and artichoke dip with the mozzarella.

7. Whisk the egg with the salt and water, then brush the dough balls with the egg wash. Cover with clingfilm (plastic wrap) and set aside in a warm place to prove for 20 minutes.

8. Meanwhile, preheat the oven to 180°C/350°F/gas 4.

9. Bake for 15–20 minutes until the dough balls are golden brown and the dips are bubbling.

BAKED BUFFALO CRACK WINGS

As the name suggests, these are very moreish. The key here is the long diffusion of salt into the chicken wings, making them taste of so much more. The last-minute brûlée of sugar balances everything out. Yum.

SERVES 4–6

2kg (4lb 6oz) good-quality chicken wings, separated into drums and flats

1½ tbsp fine sea salt

1 tbsp groundnut oil

4 tbsp hot sauce (we like Frank's)

demerara (turbinado) sugar, for sprinkling

Sauce:

250ml (generous 1 cup) hot sauce (Frank's)

100g (scant ½ cup) cold, salted butter, cubed

1. Dry the chicken wings well with kitchen paper, then toss with the salt until evenly coated. Arrange in one layer on a baking tray and refrigerate for at least 6 hours, but preferably overnight and up to 2 days. This will really dry out the skin and allow for the salt to season your chicken wings through to the bone.

2. When ready to cook, let the wings come up to room temperature for about 1 hour and preheat the oven to 200°C/400°F/gas 6.

3. Pat the wings dry again if any damp patches have developed and rub very lightly with the oil. Place, skin-side up, on a rack set over a baking tray (or 2) and bake for 40 minutes until cooked through, crisp and blistered.

4. Meanwhile, preheat the grill (broiler) to high.

5. Lightly brush each wing with the hot sauce and sprinkle evenly but confidently with the crunchy sugar. Grill (broil) for 2–3 minutes until the sugar has begun to melt onto each wing. Remove from the heat to cool slightly (the sugar will harden as it does so), then transfer to a serving platter.

6. To make the sauce, heat up the hot sauce in a small saucepan, then transfer to a blender along with the cubed butter. Blend until emulsified. Pour the sauce over your wings, leaving a few crunchy sugar bits exposed.

The Forme of Curry

The English have a deep and aromatic love affair with curry, arguably dating back to the medieval period when trade began to bring all sorts of beguiling spices to our shores. In one of the oldest English recipe books, The Forme Of Cury (disappointingly, 'Cury' means 'cookery' in Middle English and not the naan-slatherer we know and love today), we begin to see the origins of those delicately spiced dishes so adored by modern British society. One recipe calls for rabbits to be 'smyted' to pieces, browned on all sides in lard then set aside while onion purée is cooked with vinegar, sugar, cinnamon, ginger and nutmeg. The rabbit is then added back to the sauce and gently braised before being laced with cream and 'served forth'.

BUTTER CHICKEN

Butter chicken, or Murgh Makhani, is a world-famous Punjabi dish, invented at Moti Mahal in Delhi as a way to use up excess tandoori chicken. If you've got any lying around, feel free to chuck it in. Otherwise, follow this recipe. It's really good.

SERVES 4–6

Chicken/marinade:

6 fat garlic cloves, peeled

5cm (2in) piece of fresh root ginger, peeled

3 chicken breasts, sliced

juice of ½ lemon

1 tsp Kashmiri (mild) chilli powder

½ tsp ground turmeric

2 tbsp thick Greek yoghurt

1 tbsp vegetable/groundnut oil

1½ tsp flaked sea salt

Sauce:

5 tbsp neutral oil

6 green cardamom pods

2 dried bay leaves

3cm (1in) piece of cinnamon stick

½ tsp cumin seeds

1 large onion, finely chopped

2 tbsp ginger and garlic paste (see method step 1)

1½ tsp sweet smoked paprika

½ tsp ground turmeric

1 tbsp ground cumin

1½ tsp ground coriander

60g (4 tbsp) tomato purée (paste), loosened with 3 tbsp water

1 green chilli, sliced

250ml (generous 1 cup) puréed fresh tomatoes or tomato passata

200ml (generous ¾ cup) double or whipping (heavy) cream

50g (3½ tbsp) unsalted butter

2 tbsp honey, or to taste

a handful of fresh coriander (cilantro), finely chopped

1 tsp dried fenugreek leaves (kasuri methi)

lemon juice, to taste

salt, to taste

1. In a pestle and mortar, crush the garlic and ginger to a smooth paste with a little salt, then transfer to a large bowl, reserving 2 tbsp in a separate bowl for making the sauce later.

2. Add the chicken along with the rest of the marinade ingredients to the ginger/garlic paste and mix well to combine. Leave to marinate at room temperature, covered, for 1–1½ hours (no longer!).

3. To start your sauce, place a deep non-stick pan over a medium-high heat. When hot, add the oil, then throw in the whole spices. Stir them through the hot oil for 30 seconds or so until they start to change colour, then add the onion and a good pinch of salt. Cook, stirring frequently, until the onion is a light golden brown, about 10 minutes.

4. Turn the heat down a bit and add the remaining ginger/garlic paste. When the raw smell has gone, chuck in the ground spices. Briefly stir through the onion base, then add a splash of water to stop anything from catching. Tip in the tomato purée and sliced green chilli. After 1 minute or so, when the fat separates, pour in the puréed tomatoes and season with salt. Reduce over a high heat until the sauce is dry, about 5 minutes, then add the marinated chicken. Dry-fry until the meat turns white and everything is hot. Add the cream, bring back to a light simmer and cook for a few more minutes to allow the flavours to marry and the chicken to cook through. Your sauce should be a wonderful, rich shade of orange.

5. Finish the curry with the butter, honey, coriander, dried fenugreek and a squeeze of lemon. Check for salt and adjust the seasoning if you feel it needs it. It should be super-tasty and very moreish: zingy, rich, hot and a little sweet.

KEEMA RICE

Often made using mutton or lamb, keema rice is like a massive hug in a bowl. Brilliant with the roasted cumin raita on p. 120.

SERVES 4

300g (1¾ cups) basmati rice

2 tbsp oil

1 tsp cumin seeds

1 large onion, finely chopped

2 garlic cloves, minced

2 tsp minced fresh root ginger

1–2 green chillies, finely chopped

2 tbsp tomato purée (paste)

¼ tsp ground turmeric

1 tsp ground coriander

1 tsp ground cumin

½ tsp chilli powder

60g (¼ cup) tomato passata

300g (10½oz) minced (ground) beef

550ml (generous 2¼ cups) water

salt, to taste

fresh coriander (cilantro), chopped, to garnish

fresh mint, chopped, to garnish

Roasted Cumin Raita (p. 120), to serve

1. Wash the rice carefully but thoroughly (until the water runs clear), then cover with plenty of tepid water and leave to soak for 30 minutes. Drain well.

2. Meanwhile, heat the oil in a large, heavy saucepan with a lid set over a medium heat. When hot, add the cumin seeds and sauté for 30 seconds until aromatic, then add the onion along with a pinch of salt and cook, stirring, for 7–8 minutes until starting to caramelise.

3. Add the garlic, ginger, green chilli and tomato purée and cook until the raw smell has gone, then add the turmeric, coriander, cumin and chilli powder. Stir through the oil briefly, then add the passata. Reduce the heat to medium-low and cook for 5 minutes or so.

4. Turn the heat up and add the beef, breaking it up with the back of a spoon. Cook for about 10–15 minutes until the meat is cooked through and the oil starts to separate. Season with salt to taste.

5. Gently stir in the rice, then add the water and more salt to taste. Bring to the boil and cover with a circle of greaseproof paper, cover with the lid and reduce the heat to low. Cook for 10–12 minutes until the rice is cooked. Remove from the heat and let steam for 5 minutes, then remove the paper and fluff with a fork.

6. Garnish with coriander and mint, and serve with raita.

HALLOUMI SAAG

p.115

Soaking the halloumi opens out the texture of the cheese (making it remarkably similar to chicken once fried!) and draws out any excessive saltiness. Lots of sliced garlic and a sprinkling of fenugreek leaves make this a rich-tasting, earthy curry.

SERVES 4

500g (1lb 2oz) halloumi, cut into about 8 blocks

500g (1lb 2oz) spinach, washed

7 tbsp groundnut oil

1 heaped tsp cumin seeds

1 large brown onion, chopped

6 garlic cloves, halved,
then sliced widthways

4cm (1½ in) fresh root ginger, cut
into thin matchsticks

1 tsp Kashmiri (mild) chilli powder

2 tsp ground coriander

2 tsp ground cumin

½ tsp ground turmeric

200g (7oz) baby plum tomatoes,
halved or whole if small

1 green chilli, sliced

½ tsp dried fenugreek leaves
(kasuri methi), crushed to a powder
between your palms

200ml water

a pinch of garam masala

a squeeze of lemon juice, to taste

salt, to taste

double (heavy) cream,
to garnish (optional)

1. Cover the halloumi pieces with plenty of cold water and leave to soak for 1 hour (but no longer!). Drain and dry well, then set aside.

2. Meanwhile, get on with the curry. Bring a saucepan of salted water to the boil, add the spinach and briefly blanch. Drain and plunge the greens into iced water to halt the cooking, then drain again and squeeze out any excess moisture. Finely chop with a sharp knife (or pulse in a food processor) and set aside.

3. Heat 5 tbsp oil in a heavy pan over a medium-high heat and add the cumin seeds. When they splutter, throw in the chopped onion. Season with a little salt and cook, stirring frequently, until the onions are starting to brown, about 5 minutes. Add the garlic and ginger and, keeping everything moving, fry until the ginger has wilted and everything smells good (watch the garlic doesn't burn; splash a little water into the pan if it looks like it might).

4. Reduce the heat slightly and tip in the chilli powder, ground coriander, ground cumin and turmeric. Stir everything through the oil, then add another splash of water to stop anything catching. Add the tomatoes, green chilli, dried fenugreek leaves and another pinch of salt and cook until the tomatoes have wilted but not yet collapsed, about 5 minutes, topping up with a little water whenever it gets a bit dry.

5. Add the chopped spinach along with about 200ml (generous ¾ cup) water and the garam masala and bring to a gentle simmer. Cook for 10 minutes or so to bring the flavours together. The curry should be dry, with the oil starting to separate, and the tomatoes just holding their shape. Squeeze in the lemon juice and check for salt, remembering that the halloumi will be a little salty. It should be a little spicy, rich and earthy tasting. Pop the lid on and keep hot.

6. Heat the remaining 2 tbsp oil in a non-stick frying pan (skillet) and fry the halloumi slices until a deep golden brown on all sides. Don't be tempted to turn them too soon – they have a tendency to stick to the pan. Blot them briefly with kitchen paper, then gently stir them through the hot curry. Transfer to a serving dish and drizzle over the cream to garnish. Enjoy!

MANGO & FRIED CHICKPEA KACHUMBER

 p.118

Kachumber is basically an Indian chopped salad. We've added fried chickpeas (garbanzo beans), because ... *fried things*. Don't be tempted to swap the fresh curry leaves for the dried versions found in some supermarkets. Just leave them out if you can't find them.

SERVES 4

1 small red onion

2 large ripe tomatoes

⅔ cucumber

½ ripe mango

a handful of mint leaves

a handful of coriander (cilantro), stalks and all

1 green chilli, sliced (optional)

neutral oil, for frying

½ x 400g (14oz) can cooked chickpeas (garbanzo beans), rinsed, drained and thoroughly dried with kitchen paper

30 fresh curry leaves

½ tsp cumin seeds, toasted and ground

¼ tsp chilli powder

juice of 1 lemon

salt, to taste

1. Start by prepping all of the raw salad ingredients. The sizing of each component is key: you're aiming to get a bit of everything on one (heaped) tablespoon. Slice the onion very finely from root to tip. Quarter the tomatoes, then chop each quarter widthways into several chunks. Quarter the cucumber lengthways and remove the watery core, then slice on an angle about 5mm (¼in) thick. Peel the mango and slice as per the cucumber. Coarsely chop the mint and coriander. Combine everything in a large bowl with the green chilli (if using) and set aside.

2. Heat a 4cm (1½in) depth of oil in a deep heavy saucepan to 175ºC (350ºF). Working in batches, carefully lower the chickpeas into the oil and fry until very crisp and dry, about 5 minutes (watch they don't get too dark). Remove with a slotted spoon to drain briefly on kitchen paper and transfer to a small bowl. Just as the final batch of chickpeas is ready, throw in the curry leaves to crisp up (watch out – they splutter!). Drain and transfer to the bowl with the chickpeas, then toss with the cumin and chilli powders and a pinch of salt. Let cool slightly.

3. Dress everything in the salad bowl with the lemon juice and a good pinch of salt, then transfer to a shallow serving dish and top with the spicy fried chickpeas and curry leaves.

RAPID BLACK DAAL

This isn't really that rapid, but it is considerably quicker to make than the famous restaurant versions. Usually made with black urad dal (hence the distinctive colour), and slowly simmered in huge vats for up to 24 hours, ours calls for pre-cooked pulses. See? Quicker.

SERVES 4

5cm (2in) piece of fresh root ginger, peeled

6 garlic cloves, peeled

5 tbsp neutral oil

1 black cardamom pod

4 cloves

3cm (1in) piece of cinnamon stick

1 dried bay leaf

1½ tsp cumin seeds

1 large onion, chopped

1 hot green chilli, slit lengthways but left whole (optional)

½ tsp Kashmiri (mild) chilli powder

1 tsp ground coriander

½ tsp sweet smoked paprika

½ tsp paprika

80g (5 tbsp) tomato purée (paste), loosened with 3 tbsp water

1 x 400g (14oz) can cooked puy lentils, drained

1 x 400g (14oz) can black beans, drained

1 x 400g (14oz) can kidney beans, drained

½ tsp dried fenugreek leaves (kasuri methi)

100ml (scant ½ cup) double or whipping (heavy) cream

75g (⅓ cup) unsalted butter

3 tbsp finely chopped fresh coriander (cilantro)

lime juice, to taste

salt, to taste

1. In a pestle and mortar, crush the ginger and garlic to a paste with a little salt and set aside. Place a small cup of water next to your cooking station (for easy access should anything look likely to catch).

2. Place a non-stick sauté pan with a lid over a medium-high heat and, when hot, add the oil. Chuck in the whole spices and bay leaf, shortly followed by the cumin seeds. When the seeds start to crackle, add the onion, green chilli (if using) and a good pinch of salt. Cook, stirring frequently, until the onions are an even golden brown, 7–8 minutes.

3. Reduce the heat a little, then add the ginger/garlic paste and cook for 30 seconds or so until the raw smell has gone. Add the ground spices, stir through the oil to bring them to life, then dash in a bit of water to halt the cooking. Mash in the tomato purée and cook for 1 minute or so. When hot and the oil has separated, add the lentils and beans along with a very good pinch of salt, then top up with 400ml (1¾ cups) water and pop the lid on the pan. Simmer for 15–20 minutes, mashing up the beans and lentils a little as you go.

4. Crush the fenugreek leaves between your palms and sprinkle in. Simmer for a few more minutes, to allow the flavour to permeate, then stir in the cream, butter and coriander. Bring up to a simmer, then remove from the heat. Squeeze in the lime juice and check for salt. Rest for a few minutes, then serve.

ROASTED CUMIN RAITA

 p.118

There are loads of ways to make raita, that calming, yoghurt-y presence at many a curry night feast. This is our version, and it's really nice. We like to include aromatic green chilli (delicious with the roasted cumin) but if that feels counterintuitive, feel free leave it out. This really is delicious with everything.

SERVES 4

½ large cucumber

1½ tsp cumin seeds

500ml (generous 2 cups) plain yoghurt

1 green chilli, deseeded and roughly chopped

a large handful of coriander (cilantro), stalks and all

a handful of mint leaves

¼ tsp garam masala

½ garlic clove, crushed

salt, to taste

1. Coarsely grate the cucumber, season with salt and leave to drain in a sieve for 30 minutes. Squeeze out any excess moisture, then transfer to a bowl.

2. Toast the cumin seeds in a dry pan, tossing occasionally, until they start to smoke. Cool, then coarsely grind in a pestle and mortar or spice grinder. Tip into the bowl with the cucumber.

3. Chuck all the remaining ingredients into a food processor with a good pinch of salt and blend until everything is fully incorporated and smoothish.

4. Pour the yoghurt mixture over the cucumber and roasted cumin powder and mix well. Let sit for at least 30 minutes, then serve.

Boozy froyo blender lassi

 p.115

Frozen yoghurt gives this lassi a slushy-like texture, the perfect, palate-cleansing accompaniment to hotter curries. This can be scaled up to however big your blender is.

MAKES 1

3 tbsp plain Greek-style yoghurt

200g (7oz) good-quality canned mango pulp

50ml (3½ tbsp) dark rum

20ml (4 tsp) fresh lemon juice

25ml (1½ tbsp) rich demerara syrup (see method step 2)

a pinch of salt

1 cardamom pod, seeds only, freshly ground

1 small scoop crushed ice

Rich demerara syrup:

225g (generous 1 cup) demerara (turbinado) sugar

125ml (½ cup) water

Garnish:

fresh mango slices

edible flowers

chilli powder

1. Freeze the yoghurt for at least 3–4 hours or overnight before you start.

2. For the rich syrup, heat the sugar and water in a small saucepan, until the sugar has fully dissolved. Pour into a container and chill in the refrigerator until ready to use.

3. Combine the mango pulp, rum, lemon juice, the measured rich syrup, salt and ground cardamom in a blender and blend until well combined. Add the ice and blend again until fully incorporated.

4. Pour into a tall glass and garnish with fresh mango, flowers and a little sprinkle of chilli powder, if you like.

FIVE SPICES BUTTER PILAF

p.118

We make lots of pilafs at our respective homes - a great recipe to have in your repertoire. The key is in the careful treatment of the rice - be gentle and don't break the grains! The brown butter, caramelised onions and an aromatic blend of whole spices make this guy pretty special. This is a good recipe to have up your sleeve.

SERVES 4

300g (1¾ cups) good-quality basmati rice

75g (⅓ cup) unsalted butter

3cm (1in) piece of cinnamon stick

6 green cardamom pods

4 cloves

2 tsp cumin seeds

2 tsp coriander seeds

2 red onions, thinly sliced into half-moons

375ml (generous 1½ cups) hot water or stock

salt, to taste

1. Put the rice into a big bowl and gently run cold water over it until it is covered by about 5cm (2in). Carefully swirl the rice around the bowl with your hand, releasing the starch into the surrounding water. The water should turn more visibly opaque. Drain away the starchy water and repeat 5 or 6 times (sounds a lot, but it's worth it), or until you can just make out the individual grains of rice through 5cm (2in) of water. Drain a final time and cover again by 5cm (2in), but this time with tepid water. Swirl the grains gently once more to ensure an even water temperature throughout. Leave to soak for exactly 1 hour, then transfer to a sieve to drain.

2. Meanwhile, put the butter and all of the spices into a medium cast-iron pot or heavy casserole dish with a tight-fitting lid. Place over a medium-low heat and cook, stirring, until the butter has ceased foaming, is starting to brown and the spices are well toasted, about 5 minutes. Add the onions and a good pinch of salt, then reduce the heat and cook for 30–40 minutes, stirring from time to time, until the onions are very soft and nicely caramelised.

3. Add the drained rice and, using a metal tablespoon, very gently turn the grains through the fragrant butter and onions until each grain is coated. Turn the heat up a bit. After 1 minute or so, you should hear the rice sizzling in the bottom of the pot – this means it's ready for the liquid. Pour in your hot water or stock and add another pinch of salt. If any grains of rice have stuck to the side of the pot and are above the water level, quickly push them into the liquid with your spoon. Cover with a circle of greaseproof paper and the lid. Cook on the highest heat for 4 minutes, then reduce to the lowest heat for a further 7 minutes. Remove from the heat completely and leave to stand for 15 minutes with the lid on.

4. Remove and discard the greaseproof paper. Fluff through the rice with a fork and serve, making sure to snag any delicious crispy bits that have collected at the bottom of the pot.

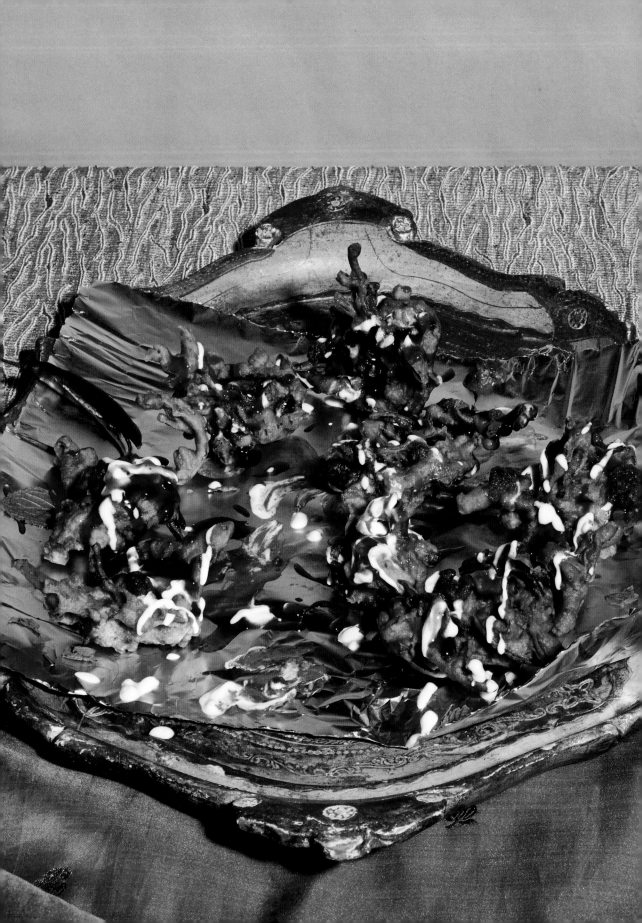

FULLY LOADED PAKORAS

Why do nachos get to have all the fun? This is a really fun one to plonk down in the middle of the table and have everyone attack. Inspired by that pre-starter, curry house amuse-bouche of poppadoms and all the sauces.

SERVES 4–6

neutral oil, for deep-frying

450g (1lb) potatoes, peeled and finely chopped into 5mm (¼in) cubes

225g (8oz) red onion (about 1 large), thinly sliced

60g (2¼oz) spinach, finely chopped

30g (1oz) fresh coriander (cilantro), chopped

1 tsp fine sea salt

2 green chillies, finely chopped

1 tbsp cumin seeds

1 tbsp ground cumin

2 tsp lightly crushed coriander seeds

1 tsp red chilli powder

300g (2½ cups) chickpea (gram) flour

2 tbsp cornflour (cornstarch)

To serve:

tamarind chutney

mint chutney

mango chutney

plain, Greek-style yoghurt

fresh coriander (cilantro)

chopped green chillies (optional)

1. Heat the oil in a deep, heavy saucepan to 175°C (350°F).

2. Meanwhile, in a large bowl, mix together the remaining pakora ingredients, adding enough water to make a batter. You want all of the vegetables to be evenly coated and just sticking together, but not at all clumpy. Mix 1 tbsp of the hot frying oil through the mixture.

3. Carefully drop heaped spoonfuls of the mixture into the hot oil and fry until golden brown, about 5 minutes.

4. Remove with a slotted spoon to drain briefly on kitchen paper, then transfer to a large platter. Drizzle over all the chutneys and the yoghurt and sprinkle with fresh coriander and green chillies.

SLOW-ROAST LAMB SHOULDER DOPIAZA

Dopiaza, a historic Moghul dish, literally means 'two' or 'double onions'. Traditionally, it features onions cooked in two different ways or at different stages of the recipe. We have honoured that, first slowly confiting the onions in the rendering fat and juices from the lamb as it slowly roasts, then puréeing some and reducing to make a wonderfully rich sauce to serve alongside.

SERVES 6

25g (1oz) fresh root ginger, peeled

25g (1oz) garlic cloves
(about ½ bulb), peeled

1 x 2kg (4lb 6oz) bone-in lamb
shoulder, at room temperature

4cm (1½in) cinnamon stick

1½ tbsp cumin seeds

2 tsp black peppercorns

4 green cardamom pods, seeds only

½ tsp ground turmeric

1 tsp Kashmiri (mild) chilli powder

250g (generous 1 cup)
thick Greek yoghurt

juice of ½ lime

3 large white onions,
sliced into half-moons

500g (1lb 6oz) tomatoes
(about 4), quartered

flaked sea salt, to taste

Sauce:

2 tbsp reserved fat from
the meat or neutral oil

1 green chilli, sliced

1 tbsp ginger and garlic paste
(see method step 1)

1 tsp ground cumin

1 tsp ground coriander

½ tsp paprika

½ tsp dried fenugreek leaves
(kasuri methi), crushed between
your palms

2 tbsp thick Greek yoghurt

3 tbsp finely chopped
coriander (cilantro)

lime juice, to taste

1. In a pestle and mortar, crush the ginger and garlic to a smooth paste with a little salt, then transfer to a bowl, reserving 1 tbsp in a separate bowl for making the sauce later.

2. Pierce the lamb shoulder all over with a small, sharp knife (to help the marinade penetrate) and season generously with salt. In a pestle and mortar or spice grinder, grind the cinnamon stick, cumin seeds, black peppercorns and cardamom seeds to a powder, then combine with the turmeric and chilli powder. Add this spice mix to the ginger/garlic paste along with the yoghurt, lime juice and another pinch of salt, then smear it all over the lamb. Marinate for at least 2 hours at room temperature (but preferably overnight in the refrigerator).

3. Preheat the oven to 230°C/450°F/gas 8.

4. Place the marinated lamb in a large, deep roasting pan and pour some water into the bottom to stop any of the marinade catching in the oven. Roast for 20–25 minutes, or until the exterior has taken on some colour, then remove and turn the heat down to 150°C/300°F/gas 2.

5. Lift out the lamb, then cover the bottom of the roasting pan with the sliced onions and quartered tomatoes and season them lightly with salt. Rest the lamb back on top, cover with greaseproof paper (to prevent anything sticking), then tightly cover with a couple of layers of foil.

6. Return to the oven for 3½ hours, or until the meat is soft and easily shreddable. Remove the lamb to a plate to rest, loosely covered with foil, while you make the sauce.

7. Strain the fat from the confit onions and tomatoes (reserving 2 tbsp for frying) and transfer everything to a blender or food processor, holding back some onions to stir through and add texture to the sauce later. Blend to a loose purée (adding a little water to help it along if necessary), then set aside.

8. For the sauce, heat the reserved lamb fat or oil in a small, non-stick saucepan, then add the green chilli. Fry briefly, then add the reserved ginger/garlic paste. When the raw smell has gone, chuck in the ground spices, stir through the fat briefly, then splash in a little water to stop anything from catching. Add all of the onion purée and dried fenugreek leaves and bring up to a light simmer. Taste for salt – it should be rich and sweet. When the sauce has reduced to your liking and the fat has started to separate, stir through the reserved confit onions and bring back to a simmer.

9. Remove from the heat and stir through the yoghurt, chopped coriander and lime juice, to taste. Serve alongside the lamb at the table.

CHICKEN 65

As is the case with popular dishes (especially when the name is this cool), many myths have spawned about Chicken 65's true origins. They're all great. One affirms that the chicken must be exactly 65 days old when butchered. Another that the original recipe included 65 different chillies. We just love the name. Oh, and these are incredible with loads of cold beers.

SERVES 4–6

450g (1lb) boneless chicken thighs, cut into bite-size pieces

neutral oil, for deep-frying

1 small red onion, cut into rings, to garnish

Batter/marinade:

80g (⅓ cup) Greek yoghurt

2 garlic cloves, minced

1 tsp minced fresh root ginger

1 egg

2 tbsp red chilli powder

1 tsp ground coriander

½ tsp ground turmeric

50g (½ cup) cornflour (cornstarch)

1 tbsp water

2 tsp fine sea salt

Temper:

2 tbsp oil

1 tsp cumin seeds

25 fresh curry leaves

3 green chillies, finely chopped

2 garlic cloves, finely chopped

2 tsp sugar

2 tsp soy sauce

1. In a large bowl, combine the batter/marinade ingredients. Fold through the chicken and set aside, covered, for at least 30 minutes or for up to 24 hours.

2. Heat the oil in a deep, heavy saucepan to 175°C (350°F). Working in batches, carefully lift the individual pieces of chicken out of the marinade/batter and to the oil. Fry until golden brown, 3–4 minutes. Remove with a slotted spoon to drain briefly on kitchen paper.

3. For the temper, heat the oil in a separate pan. Add the cumin seeds and, when they splutter, add the curry leaves, green chillies and garlic and fry until aromatic. Add the sugar and soy sauce, shortly followed by the fried chicken pieces. Toss well to combine, ensuring everything is hot, then transfer to a serving platter and garnish with sliced red onions.

Hungover Saturday Breakfast

A Roman Hangover

Maybe more than any other empire, the Romans loved to party. With feasts full of wine, sow's udders, stuffed dormice and flamingo tongues, the morning after a night at Caesar's Palace obviously required some serious consideration. Small wonder that their hungover breakfasts were extremely elaborate. According to Pliny the Elder, the famous nature-loving pseudoscientist, overindulgence was best cured by deep-frying an unlucky canary and scoffing it whole. Strangely, there has been very little contemporary research into whether or not this actually works.

FRENCH TOAST PATTY MELT

French toast, eggy bread, pain perdu, poor knights of Windsor … whatever you call it, it's a good choice for breakfast. But so is a patty melt, which is basically a grilled cheese with a burger and loads of onions in it. Great if you're feeling a little indecisive and seriously worse for wear.

MAKES 3

2 eggs

125ml (½ cup) whole (full-fat) milk

400g (14oz) good-quality freshly minced (ground) beef (at least 15% fat)

neutral oil, for frying

6 slices of sourdough or rye bread

300g (10½oz) sharp, nutty Swiss cheese, grated

4 tbsp unsalted butter

salt and freshly ground black pepper, to taste

Caramelised onions:

1 tbsp neutral oil

2 tbsp unsalted butter

3 large white onions, thinly sliced from root to tip

a pinch of salt

1 tsp caraway seeds

water or beef stock, for deglazing

1. Heat the oil and butter in a heavy stainless steel or cast-iron pan over a medium heat until foaming and go in with the onions, a good pinch of salt and the caraway seeds. Cook your onions for about 45 minutes, stirring occasionally (sounds a long time, but it's worth it). Whenever you see brown sediment catching at the bottom of the pan, deglaze with a tbsp or so of water or stock and draw it through the onions, allowing the moisture to evaporate and the process to start all over again. This residue is where all the flavour is rooted, so watch it doesn't get too dark or the onions will taste bitter or burnt. When they're ready they should be rich, dark brown, sweet and spreadable. Tip into a bowl and set aside to cool.

2. In a shallow bowl, whisk together the eggs and milk with a good pinch of salt and pepper. Set aside.

3. Carefully shape the beef into patties, trying not to work the meat too much. They should be about 1.5cm (½in) thick.

4. Preheat a frying pan/skillet (cast iron is good) over a medium-high heat and coat the bottom with oil. When smoking, season your patties well with salt and pepper and fry, without moving, for 1½ minutes or so, to get a good crust on them. Flip and continue cooking for 30 seconds or so, or until medium-rare, then remove from the pan.

5. Grab a piece of bread and top with a good amount of grated cheese, a cooked patty, a solid schmear of caraway onions, more cheese, then the second piece of bread.

6. Preheat the oven to 220°C/425°F/gas 7.

7. Foam the butter in an ovenproof frying pan. Dunk each sandwich in the egg mixture – it should only just submerge the bottom slice. Flip and repeat with the other side. Fry until browned on both sides, then transfer to a baking tray and bake in the oven until oozy, crunchy and delicious.

CHEAT'S HANGOVER CARBONARA

When your head's pounding, you don't want to fuss around with raw eggs. This is one of our mum's recipes.

SERVES 4

250g (9oz) unsmoked fatty bacon lardons or pancetta

1 large onion, chopped

1 heaped tbsp unsalted butter

2 garlic cloves, thinly sliced

1 heaped tsp freshly ground black pepper

a fat pinch of chilli flakes

250g (9oz) mascarpone cheese

400g (14oz) spaghetti

50g (¾ cup) Parmesan, grated, plus extra to serve

3 tbsp finely chopped flat-leaf parsley

salt, to taste

1. Set a non-stick sauté pan over a medium heat and add the bacon lardons. Once they have rendered their fat and are a bit crisp, tip in the chopped onion and season lightly with salt. Reduce the heat and cook very gently for 15 minutes, stirring occasionally and being careful not to brown the onions. You want them to be sweet and translucent.

2. Turn the heat up a bit and add the butter, garlic, black pepper and the chilli flakes. When everything smells nice and the garlic is sticky but not brown, splash in a little hot water then stir through the mascarpone. Taste for salt, bearing in mind you are yet to add the Parmesan. Keep the sauce warm.

3. Cook your pasta in plenty of salted boiling water until al dente, according to the packet instructions. Drain, reserving some of the pasta cooking water, then transfer to the sauce. Add a good splash of the reserved pasta water, along with the Parmesan and parsley. Toss very well, adding more pasta water to loosen if necessary. Serve with extra Parmesan.

 Wasabi bloody Mary **p.136**

Bloody Marys are a question of taste – a sinus-cleansing amount of wasabi is key in our opinion, but feel free to adjust.

MAKES 1

1 tbsp teriyaki sauce

2 tsp pickled ginger brine

1½ tsp miso paste

2 tsp wasabi paste

1 tsp shichimi togarashi (Japanese 7-spice blend) (or a mix of 1 tsp toasted sesame seeds, 1 tsp mild chilli powder and ½ tsp ground ginger)

½ tsp freshly ground black pepper

4 tsp lime juice

2 generous tbsp vodka

1 tbsp sake (or more vodka)

250ml (1 cup) tomato juice, chilled

salt, to taste

To serve:

lime wedge

½ tsp salt

½ tsp freshly ground black pepper

1 tsp shichimi togarashi

ice cubes

pickled ginger

1. Combine the teriyaki sauce, pickled ginger brine, miso, wasabi, shichimi togarashi, pepper and salt to taste in a cocktail tin/glass shaker and stir to mix well. This is your base.

2. Add the lime juice, vodka, sake (if using) and tomato juice. Fit the other half of the cocktail tin/glass shaker and 'roll' the mixture back and forth several times, until well combined.

3. Take a fresh glass and wet the rim with a lime wedge. Combine the salt, pepper and togarashi in a saucer and dip the edge of the glass into the mixture to coat the rim. Fill the glass with ice and pour the cocktail over.

4. Garnish with pickled ginger and serve with whatever deep-fried Japanese snacks you happen to have lying around.

INDIAN SCRAMBLED EGGS

p.133

This is our version of a Mumbai street-food classic, egg bhurji. As with most street-food dishes, the old cliché rings true: there are as many versions as there are chefs. Just as quick and easy as regular scrambled eggs (well, not really, but definitely more delicious).

SERVES 4

1 tbsp unsalted butter

2½ tsp cumin seeds

1 medium red onion, diced

1–2 green chillies, chopped

180g (6½oz) plum tomatoes, diced

1½ tsp ground coriander

¼ tsp ground turmeric

½ tsp chilli powder

8 large eggs

2 tbsp milk

a handful of fresh coriander (cilantro), chopped, plus extra to serve

salt, to taste

buttered toast, rotis or naan bread, to serve

1. Heat the butter in a non-stick pan over a medium heat. Add the cumin seeds and, when aromatic, add the onion and cook for about 5 minutes, stirring frequently, until translucent but not brown. Add the green chilli and tomatoes and cook for a further 2 minutes, then add the ground spices, mix well and cook for 3 minutes.

2. Reduce the heat to medium-low. Whisk the eggs together with the milk and pour into the pan. Cook, stirring with a spatula, until the eggs begin to scramble. Season with salt, then fry for an additional 2 minutes until slightly dry. Remove from the heat and fold in the coriander.

3. Serve with generously buttered rotis or toast.

FRY-UP FRIED RICE

 p.136

The perfect way to use up leftover takeout rice. Great with hash browns, beans, buttered toast and a cuppa.

SERVES 4

1 tbsp oyster sauce

2 tbsp tomato ketchup

2 tbsp light soy sauce

1 tsp sesame oil

2 tbsp vegetable or sunflower oil

8 rashers smoked bacon, diced

3 sausages, casings removed

a large handful of shiitake mushrooms, sliced

2 garlic cloves, finely chopped

4 spring onions (scallions), sliced, plus extra to serve

3 large eggs, beaten

600g (4½ cups) cooked long-grain rice (about 200g/generous 1 cup uncooked), chilled

½ tsp freshly ground black pepper

salt, to taste

1. Whisk together the oyster sauce, ketchup, soy sauce and sesame oil in a bowl and set aside.

2. Get a wok or large saucepan ripping hot, add 1 tbsp of the oil and chuck in the diced bacon. Fry until the bacon fat has rendered and it is a bit crisp, then remove with a slotted spoon and set aside.

3. Fry the sausagemeat in the bacon fat until crisp, breaking it up into small pieces as you do so. Remove and set aside with the bacon.

4. Add the mushrooms to the residual pork fat, season with a little salt and fry until the moisture has evaporated and they have taken on some colour. Set aside.

5. Add the remaining 1 tbsp oil to the pan and add the garlic, moving it through the oil briefly before adding the spring onions and a little pinch of salt. Pour in the whisked eggs, allow to set for a few seconds, then roughly scramble around the wok or pan. Throw in the cooked rice and toss well. Return the bacon, sausage and mushrooms to the pan and continue moving everything around the pan for a few minutes. When it is all sizzling hot, add the sauce and the black pepper and toss to ensure everything is nicely coated.

6. Transfer to a serving dish and top with more sliced spring onions.

HAM & MUSHROOM CROQUE MADAME

'Croque Madame' essentially translates to 'Mrs Crunch'. When cooked correctly this sublime sarnie should be crisp on the outside then give way to the molten velvet loveliness of béchamel, ham and mushroom. The perfect thing to crawl out of bed for on a Saturday morning.

SERVES 4

8 slices of sourdough bread

2 tbsp unsalted butter

8 thick slices of ham

300g (2⅔ cups) Gruyère cheese, shredded

2 tsp oil

4 eggs

salt and freshly ground black pepper, to taste

Béchamel:

2 tbsp unsalted butter

3 tbsp plain (all-purpose) flour

300ml (generous 1¼ cups) whole (full-fat) milk

1 tbsp Dijon mustard

50g (¾ cup) Parmesan, finely grated

salt and freshly ground black pepper, to taste

Mushrooms:

1 tbsp unsalted butter

2 shallots, finely chopped

½ tsp thyme leaves

400g (14oz) mushrooms, sliced

1 garlic clove, finely chopped

salt and freshly ground black pepper, to taste

1. For the Béchamel, melt the butter in a small saucepan over a medium heat. Whisk in the flour and cook for 2–3 minutes, stirring constantly. Gradually pour in the milk, stirring to combine, until the sauce is thickened and smooth. Stir in the mustard and Parmesan. Season with salt and pepper to taste and transfer to a bowl to cool.

2. For the filling, melt the butter in a large frying pan (skillet) over a medium-high heat. Add the shallots and cook for about 5 minutes until softened. Add the thyme and mushrooms and cook for about 10 minutes, stirring occasionally, until the mushrooms are caramelised, then add the garlic and cook, stirring, for about 30 seconds until fragrant. Season with salt and pepper to taste.

3. Preheat the grill (broiler) to high and the oven to 200°C/400°F/gas 6.

4. Spread the bread with butter on one side and arrange, buttered-side up, on a baking tray. Grill (broil) the bread until just golden brown, then let cool.

5. When cooled, spread the untoasted side of 4 slices of bread with some of the béchamel sauce. Top each with two slices of ham, some of the mushroom mixture and top with half of the Gruyère cheese. Top with the remaining slices of bread, toasted-side up, then add a final layer of béchamel and Gruyère cheese. Bake in the oven for about 10 minutes until golden and bubbling.

6. Meanwhile, heat the oil in a non-stick frying pan (skillet) over a low-medium heat. Crack in the eggs, leaving a little space in between, season with salt and pepper and fry until the tops of the whites are set but the yolks are still a little runny.

7. Top each sandwich with a fried egg and serve immediately.

CACIO E PEPE BISCUIT SANDWICHES

Before we get embroiled in a pedantic, pan-Atlantic fist fight over the correct usage of the word 'biscuit', let's all just agree to disagree. In this instance, the biscuit is less Hobnob, more crumbly, savoury, scone-like rolls. These sandwiches are inspired by Cacio e Pepe, the latest creamy Roman pasta sauce to take the culinary world by storm. Rich and nutty from the Pecorino cheese (Parmesan is fine, too), with a welcome warming hit of black pepper.

SERVES 6

450g (3½ cups) plain (all-purpose) flour, plus extra for dusting

2½ tsp baking powder

¼ tsp bicarbonate of soda (baking soda)

1 tbsp sugar

2 tsp fine sea salt

1 tbsp coarsely ground black pepper, plus extra to serve

225g (1 cup) cold, unsalted butter, cut into cubes, plus 60g (¼ cup) melted

35g (½ cup) grated Pecorino cheese

85g (1 cup) Double Gloucester cheese, grated

235ml (1 cup) buttermilk, chilled

Filling:

2 tbsp olive oil

12 rashers bacon, cut in half

8 eggs

60ml (¼ cup) milk

½ tsp fine sea salt

½ tsp freshly ground black pepper

2 tbsp unsalted butter

2 tbsp finely chopped chive

ketchup, or other condiments (optional)

1. Put the flour, baking powder, bicarbonate of soda, sugar, salt and pepper into a food processor and pulse to combine. Add the cubed butter and pulse until the butter pieces are the size of peas.

2. Transfer to a bowl, add the cheeses and drizzle over the buttermilk. Use a fork to roughly combine, then turn out onto a lightly floured work surface and gently work together into a shaggy dough.

3. Pat the dough into a rectangle and fold into thirds, then flatten back into a rectangle. Repeat this process twice, then pat into a 3cm (1in) thick rectangle. Dust a sharp knife with flour and cut the dough into 6 equal square pieces. Arrange on a baking tray lined with baking paper and chill in the refrigerator for 30 minutes.

4. Preheat the oven to 220°C/425°F/gas 7.

5. Meanwhile, heat the olive oil in a non-stick frying pan (skillet) over a medium heat and fry the bacon until nicely crisp and delicious. Set aside to drain on kitchen paper and wipe the pan clean.

6. Remove the biscuits from the refrigerator and brush with the melted butter. Bake for 20 minutes until golden on top, then transfer to a wire rack to cool.

7. Meanwhile, whisk together the eggs, milk, salt and pepper in a large bowl. Melt the butter in the frying pan over a medium-low heat, add the eggs and stir slowly to combine and cook through until nicely scrambled. Don't rush this – you want them good and creamy.

8. To serve, break the biscuits in half, and cram with the eggs and crispy bacon. Serve with ketchup, or other condiments, as desired.

GIANT BREAKFAST CRUNCHWRAP

This is essentially a massive round breakfast burrito, but without all the filler – a great option if you've hit it hard the night before. Once turned out, you can slice this like a cake, dunking the slices into your favourite breakfast condiments like a boss.

SERVES 6–8

1 x 700g (1lb 9oz) packet
ready-made hash browns

4 sausages

12 rashers bacon

8 eggs

2 tbsp milk

2 tsp unsalted butter, plus 1 tbsp
melted for brushing

2 tbsp chopped chives

7 large flour tortillas

180g (2 cups) Cheddar, grated

salt and freshly ground black
pepper, to taste

1. Preheat the oven to 180°C/350°F/gas 4 and the grill (broiler) to medium-high.

2. Bake the hash browns according to the packet directions.

3. Meanwhile, cook the sausages by your preferred method and slice into rounds. Likewise, cook the bacon until crispy.

4. Whisk together the eggs and milk and season with salt and pepper.

5. Heat the 2 tsp butter in a non-stick saucepan over a medium-low heat. Pour in the eggs and cook, stirring occasionally, until just cooked and nicely scrambled. Fold through the chives and remove from the heat.

6. Brush a 30cm (12in) round cast-iron skillet or ovenproof frying pan with melted butter. Arrange 5 tortillas, overlapping, around the edge of the pan and place 1 in the middle to form a base. Sprinkle over half of the cheese and place the hash browns on top, then cover with the scrambled eggs, sausage slices, bacon and the remaining cheese. Place the remaining tortilla on top and then fold over the edges of the overlapping tortillas to cover and form a sort of parcel.

7. Top with a piece of greaseproof paper and weigh it down with something flat and heavy (to stop the wraps from unfurling) and place in the oven for 20–25 minutes, or until golden brown.

8. Remove the crunchwrap from the pan and flip over, then place under the grill until golden brown.

9. Serve with your favourite breakfast condiments.

CALABRIAN EGGS, FRIED SLICE

Nduja, an amazing spicy, spreadable sausage from Calabria, is heady with the aroma of chillies, very versatile and completely worth seeking out. They vary in spiciness, so do investigate before you throw the full amount in. Or put more in! It's up to you. We suppose, at a push, you could substitute chorizo here, or even some harissa in an attempt to keep it vegetarian. Less good, perhaps, but not bad at all. Fried slice FTW.

....

SERVES 4

3 tbsp olive oil, or more
as necessary

2 red onions, sliced into
thin half-moons

1 red chilli, sliced

2 garlic cloves, crushed
to a paste with a little salt

100g (3½oz) nduja
(soft, spicy Calabrian sausage)

2 x 400g (14oz) cans nice
plum tomatoes

½ tsp sugar

4 eggs

4 slices of white bread

unsalted butter (or olive oil),
for frying

grated Pecorino or Parmesan,
to serve

Gremolata:

½ small bunch of flat-leaf parsley,
very finely chopped

½ small bunch of mint, very
finely chopped

1 garlic clove, very finely chopped

zest of 1 lemon

salt, to taste

1. Heat 3 tbsp olive oil in a heavy sauté pan (with a lid) over a medium heat. Add the onions and red chilli along with a pinch of salt, then reduce the heat a little and cook for about 30 minutes, stirring frequently, until very soft, sweet and lightly caramelised.

2. Create a little room in the middle of your pan and add the crushed garlic along with another 1 tsp oil if it needs it. Cook until it smells fragrant, then tip in the nduja. Break up the sausage with the side of a spoon, mashing it through the onions and garlic, ensuring everything is hitting the oil and is frying evenly. Crush the tomatoes in a bowl with your hands, then chuck into the pan along with the sugar. Season warily with salt (nduja can vary in saltiness), then simmer gently for 30 minutes, partially covered with the lid. Top up with a little water if it's looking a bit dry at any stage.

3. For the gremolata, mix the chopped herbs and garlic with the lemon zest and set aside.

4. Turn the heat down on the tomato sauce and crack the eggs into the pan, dragging a fork through the whites a little (this encourages them to cook at the same time as the yolks). Season lightly with salt, cover with a lid and cook for about 8 minutes.

5. While the eggs are cooking, fry the sliced bread in butter (or olive oil) on both sides until crisp and golden brown. Drain on kitchen paper, then lay on your serving plates. Top the fried slices with a good spoonful of tomato sauce and an egg each. Finish with plenty of cheese and the gremolata. Dig in.

Christmas Party

Krampusnacht

All kids know that bad behaviour means coal for Christmas. Though this prospect is enough to keep most children in line, Germanic legend takes things to terrifying new extremes. Instead of an angry Saint Nick, naughty Austrian kinders are confronted with a horrifying embodiment of Christmas evil – the dreaded Krampus. According to myth, this half-goat, half-demon monster spends each festive season prowling and patrolling Teutonic streets on the hunt for anyone unfortunate enough to have misbehaved in the previous year. Those who cross his path are then picked up and carted off to the underworld. The only way to prevent this fate is to placate the Krampus with copious shots of cold peach schnapps.

MONTE CRISTO FINGER SANDWICHES

A disowned member of the croque monsieur family, this filthy sandwich shot to fame in 1930s America. We've tweaked the original and reimagined it at an afternoon tea. Don't hold back with the sugar – embrace it.

MAKES 9–12

6 slices of good white bread, crusts removed

salted butter, for spreading

mayonnaise, for spreading

6 thin slices of mortadella

250g (generous 2 cups) Comté cheese, grated

250g (1½ cups) cooked turkey breast, shredded or sliced

groundnut or rapeseed oil, for frying

icing (confectioners') sugar, for dusting

Batter:

200g (1½ cups) plain (all-purpose) flour

50g (½ cup) cornflour (cornstarch)

1 tsp baking powder

⅓ nutmeg, grated

1 tsp fine sea salt

1 tsp freshly ground black pepper

2 large eggs

350ml (1½ cups) whole (full-fat) milk, cold

1. Lightly toast the bread and liberally spread one side of each slice with butter and then mayonnaise. Build the filling on 3 of these dressed slices. Layer up 1 folded slice of mortadella, then a few pinches of grated cheese, some sliced turkey, more cheese and then a second slice of mortadella. Top each with the remaining dressed pieces of toast, with the dressed side facing down. Weigh the sandwiches down with something flat and heavy for 15 minutes or so.

2. Meanwhile, heat a 5cm (2in) depth of oil in a deep heavy saucepan to 175°C (350°F).

3. For the batter, combine the flours, baking powder, nutmeg, salt and pepper in a bowl and separately whisk together the eggs and milk. Slowly add the wet ingredients to the dry, whisking and trying to eliminate any lumps as you go (but don't worry too much if there are a few small ones). The batter should be slightly thicker than the consistency of double (heavy) cream.

4. Remove the weight and slice each sandwich into 3 or 4 fingers (how many you cut will depend on the size of your bread – you choose!). Dunk each 'finger' into the batter, then immediately lower into the hot oil, without allowing too much batter to drip off. Fry the fingers for 3–4 minutes until golden brown and crunchy, turning often with a slotted spoon to ensure even cooking.

5. Remove to a rack to drain and cool slightly, then dust liberally with icing sugar. Enjoy!

CHOCOLATE HAZELNUT CHRISTMAS TREE

Christmas wouldn't be Christmas without a dying tree sitting in your house surrounded by pressies. Why not make a pastry version of it and stuff it with everyone's favourite hazelnut-flavoured chocolate spread? Considering this only uses a few ingredients, takes about five minutes to prepare and is eminently Instagrammable, why not indeed?

SERVES 8

2 x sheets ready rolled puff pastry, chilled

150g (½ cup) chocolate hazelnut spread (such as Nutella)

1 egg, beaten with a little salt

icing (confectioners') sugar, for dusting

1. Preheat the oven to 190°C/375°F/gas 5. Line a very large baking tray with baking paper.

2. Lay out one sheet of pastry on the lined tray. Spread over the chocolate hazelnut spread in a rough triangle shape.

3. Place the second sheet of pastry on top of the first, then cut out a triangle shape (as close as you can get to the size of the spread section) with a small trunk at the bottom. Discard the trimmings.

4. Make even horizontal cuts through both layers of pastry at regular intervals down both sides of the triangle, leaving about 5cm (2in) uncut in the middle, to hold the tree together.

5. Twist each strip along its length to create tree branches.

6. Brush the pastry all over with the beaten egg.

7. Bake for 20–25 minutes, or until well-risen and golden brown.

8. Dust with icing sugar, and enjoy!

 Chocolate orange liqueur p.152

A quick and easy last-minute pressie idea. A little (thought) goes a long way.

MAKES 750ML/3¼ CUPS

200ml (generous ¾ cup) double (heavy) cream

150g (1¼ cups) icing (confectioners') sugar, sifted

4 tbsp cocoa powder

the pared zest of 3–4 oranges

100ml (generous ⅓ cup) orange juice

100g (3½oz) dark chocolate (70%), chopped

200ml (generous ¾ cup) dark rum

1. Add the cream, icing sugar, cocoa, orange zests and juice to a large saucepan and stir to combine over a low heat. Gradually add the chocolate until fully incorporated. When the mixture is glossy and smooth, remove from the heat and stir through the rum. Cover and leave to infuse and cool completely.

2. The longer you leave the mixture before straining, the zestier it becomes, but by the time it is cool the orange zest should have done its work. Pass through a fine sieve and transfer to a sterilised bottle. It keeps well chilled for 2 weeks or so.

JALEPEÑO POPPER MAC 'N' CHEESE NUGGETS

 p.149

These deep-fried squares of cheesy perfection are the perfect precursor to a huge roast turkey dinner.

SERVES 8

350g (12oz) dried elbow macaroni

1.15l (5 cups) whole (full-fat) milk

350g (12oz) mature
Cheddar, grated

40g (⅔ cup) Parmesan,
finely grated

200g (scant 1 cup) cream cheese

8 bacon rashers, chopped and
fried until crisp (optional)

130g (4½oz) pickled jalapeños,
finely chopped

100g (¾ cup) plain
(all-purpose) flour

4 eggs, beaten with a little milk

200g (4½ cups) panko breadcrumbs

salt and freshly ground
black pepper

1. Combine the macaroni and milk in a large saucepan and bring to a gentle simmer, stirring all the time. Season with salt to taste.

2. After 15–20 minutes the macaroni will have absorbed some of the milk and should be tender and the remaining milk will have thickened to the texture of double (heavy) cream. If it's too thick, add a little hot water.

3. Remove from the heat and leave to stand for a few minutes (if you are too hasty, the cheeses can split and become grainy). When it has cooled a little stir in the cheeses, bacon and jalapeños and season with salt and pepper to taste.

4. Pour the mixture into a deep baking tray lined with clingfilm (plastic wrap) and smooth out the top. Refrigerate for about 1 hour – it needs to be pretty solid for the next step.

5. Remove the set mixture and cut it into 4cm (1½in) squares, or thereabouts.

6. Place the flour and egg wash in separate shallow bowls. Place the panko in another shallow bowl and season with 1 tsp salt. Dip the squares first in the flour, shaking off any excess, then into the egg wash, letting any excess drip back into the bowl, then in the breadcrumbs. Make sure each square is completely covered; any gaps will let the filling melt into the oil and burn during frying.

7. Heat the oil in a deep, heavy saucepan to 175ºC (350ºF). Fry the nuggets in batches of 5 or so until the coating is golden brown and crispy, about 5 minutes. Remove with a slotted spoonto drain on kitchen paper.

CRISPY ONION GLAZED SAUSAGES

 p.152

The original awkward family Christmas party nibble. Great eaten while manoeuvering small talk fuelled by lots of cheap prosecco.

SERVES 8

12 Cumberland sausages

2 shallots, thinly sliced into
half-moons

groundnut or rapeseed oil,
for cooking

Glaze:

2½ tbsp wholegrain mustard

3 tbsp American mustard

6 tbsp honey

1 heaped tsp Marmite
(or other yeast extract spread)

a good pinch of cayenne pepper

Dip:

150ml (⅔ cup) sour cream

4 tbsp chopped chives

salt, to taste

1. Preheat the oven to 200ºC/400ºF/gas 6.

2. Pinch each sausage in the middle and twist several times to create 2 mini sausages. Rub with about 1 tsp of the oil and place in a roasting pan. Roast for 20–25 minutes, or until the sausages have taken on some colour and are cooked through.

3. Meanwhile, put the shallots in a small saucepan and pour in enough cold oil to just cover. Place over a medium heat and bring up to frying temperature, stirring occasionally to encourage even cooking. The shallots are ready when they are an even, light golden brown. Watch they don't colour too much as they can easily become bitter. Equally, these tend to crisp up very well once out of the oil, so don't worry if they are not super-crispy when still in the oil! Use a slotted spoon to transfer to kitchen paper to drain.

4. Combine all the ingredients for the glaze in a non-stick saucepan and cook over a medium heat until slightly reduced. Snip the roasted sausages at each twist to separate them, then toss through the glaze. Tip the lot into a serving bowl (along with any excess glaze) and pile your crispy onions on top.

5. Mix together the dip ingredients and serve on the side.

CAMEMBERT SNOWFLAKE

Less of a recipe and more of a pastry hack, this is a relatively quick, easy and anxiety-free way to impress people at a party. Camembert, that darling of viral food content, is the star of the show here, nestled in the middle of this rippable piece of interactive food art. After all, nothing really says Christmas like cheese, chutney and snowflakes.

SERVES 8

2 x sheets ready rolled puff pastry

1 x 300g (10½oz) jar chutney of your choice

1 Camembert, still in its fancy wooden box but with any plastic wrapping removed

1 egg, beaten

flaked sea salt, to taste

2 large rosemary sprigs, cut into smaller sprigs

1–2 garlic cloves, cut into thin slivers (optional)

1. Preheat the oven to 180°C/350°F/gas 4. Line a very large baking tray or cookie sheet with baking paper.

2. Cut the pastry sheets into 2 equal-sized circles, as large as you can get from the sheets. Lay the first circle of pastry on the lined tray and liberally spread chutney in a ring around the edge, leaving a Camembert-sized circle in the middle.

3. Lay the second sheet of puff pastry on top of the first.

4. Place the Camembert in its box right in the middle of the pastry circle. Using the box as a template, cut around it, then remove the circle of excess pastry from beneath it. Imagine the circle of pastry as a clock face. Make 4 cuts through both layers of pastry, stopping about 1cm (½in) short of the Camembert, at 12 o'clock, 3 o'clock, 6 o'clock and 9 o'clock. Make a further 3 cuts in each quarter in the same way, creating a total of 16 spokes.

5. Using both hands, take 2 adjacent spokes of pastry and twist them in opposite directions away from each other, giving them each a couple of turns. Brush the ends of each spoke with egg wash and pinch the pair together. Do the same with all the other adjacent spokes – it should start looking like a snowflake at this point.

6. Remove the Camembert. Brush the whole pastry with egg wash and scatter with sea salt. Bake for 15 minutes, then remove from the oven.

7. Make a few cuts in the Camembert and insert the rosemary sprigs and slivered garlic. Place the boxed cheese back in the hole in the middle of the pastry snowflake and return to the oven to bake for a further 20 minutes, until the pastry is puffed up and golden and the cheese feels as though it has melted inside. Be careful – if you cook it too much, Camembert is prone to going a bit strange.

8. Transfer to a platter and get stuck in.

CORONATION TURKEY-STUFFED DOUGH BALLS

This is deliciously, unashamedly retro. It's essentially a riff on that classic denizen of Boxing Day, the traditional leftover turkey curry, with a Coronation chicken twist. The '70s in a dough ball.

SERVES 10

1 x Milk Buns recipe (p.22)

2 tsp oil

1 onion, diced

2 garlic cloves, minced

2 tsp grated fresh root ginger

1 green chilli, finely chopped

1½ tbsp curry powder

500g (3 cups) cooked, shredded turkey

200ml (generous ¾ cup) coconut milk

100g (½ cup) plain Greek-style yoghurt

2 tbsp mango chutney

zest and juice of ½ lemon

40g (¼ cup) raisins

2 tbsp chopped fresh coriander (cilantro)

1 egg

2 tsp milk

nigella seeds, for sprinkling

salt and freshly ground black pepper, to taste

1. First make your milk bread dough according to steps 1–4 of the recipe on **p.22** (it will need at least 1 hour to rise).

2. Heat the oil in a large saucepan over a medium heat, add the onion and sauté until translucent, about 5 minutes. Stir in the garlic and ginger and cook for 1 minute until aromatic.

3. Add the green chilli and curry powder and cook briefly until the rawness of the spices has gone. Splash in a little water if anything looks like it might catch. Fold through the turkey ensuring it is well coated, then add the coconut milk, yoghurt, mango chutney, lemon juice and zest, and raisins. Continue cooking until it comes to a simmer, then remove from the heat.

4. Fold through the coriander and season with salt and pepper to taste. Set aside to cool.

5. Divide the dough into golf ball-sized pieces. Flatten and place a heaped tbsp of the turkey filling in the middle of each round. Bring up the sides of the dough to enclose and pinch closed. Roll the bottom of each to seal gently into round balls. Arrange on a baking tray lined with baking paper and cover with clingfilm (plastic wrap) or a dry cloth. Let rise in a warm place for 30–40 minutes until the dough has doubled in size.

6. Meanwhile, preheat the oven to 200ºC/400ºF/gas 6.

7. Mix the egg and milk together. Brush the dough balls with the egg wash and sprinkle with nigella seeds.

8. Bake for 15–20 minutes until golden brown.

9. Let them cool slightly on the tray, then enjoy!

FRIED STUFFING BALLS & GRAVY DIP

You're standing by the buffet at a Christmas party. You're drunk, nobody is talking to you and you've got red wine and some unidentified sauce down your Xmas jumper. Something catches your eye from the depths of your festive misery, something deep-fried and delicious. You take one of the lovely crispy balls in your hand, dip it in the accompanying gravy and the smell of orange zest and chestnuts transports you to somewhere far away. Suddenly, everything is going to be OK.

SERVES 8

2 tbsp unsalted butter

2 medium brown onions, very finely diced

2 garlic cloves, crushed

2 Granny Smith apples, peeled and finely diced

20 sage leaves, finely chopped

600g (1lb 5oz) good-quality sausagemeat

4 slices of white bread, toasted until crisp, then blitzed into breadcrumbs

100g (3½oz) cooked chestnuts, crumbled

zest of 1 orange

½ nutmeg, grated

1 tbsp flaked sea salt

1 tbsp freshly ground black pepper

200g (1½ cups) plain (all-purpose) flour

4 eggs, beaten with a splash of milk

200g (4½ cups) panko breadcrumbs

2l (8½ cups) groundnut oil

Gravy dip:

1 tbsp unsalted butter

2 tbsp plain (all-purpose) flour

100ml (generous ⅓ cup) white wine

200ml (generous ¾ cup) top-quality chicken stock

salt and freshly ground black pepper, to taste

1. For the stuffing balls, heat the butter in a frying pan (skillet) until sizzling, add the onions and gently fry until soft. Add the garlic and fry for a further 30 seconds, then add the chopped apple and a splash of water and cook for a further 15 minutes until the apple pieces have softened and the water has evaporated. Stir in the sage leaves, then remove the mixture to a bowl and leave to cool.

2. When cool enough to handle, mix with the sausagemeat, breadcrumbs, chestnuts, orange zest, nutmeg, salt and pepper. Refrigerate for 1 hour.

3. Place the flour, beaten eggs and panko breadcrumbs in separate bowls.

4. Mould the stuffing mixture into walnut-sized balls. Dip them one at a time into the flour, shaking off any excess, then into the eggs, allowing the excess to drip back into the bowl, and then into the panko, rolling them around to obtain a thorough coating.

5. Heat the oil in a deep, heavy saucepan to 175°C (350°F).

6. While the oil heats up, make the gravy dip. Heat the butter in a small saucepan until foaming, then whisk in the flour. Gradually pour in the white wine, stirring to make a smooth paste, then do the same with the stock. Strain through a sieve to remove any lumps, then return to the pan and gently simmer to reduce to your desired consistency. Season to taste.

7. Fry the stuffing balls in the hot oil in batches of 6 or so, until golden brown. Remove with a slotted spoon to a tray lined with kitchen paper, then to a wire cooling rack to stop them going soggy. Serve with the gravy on the side.

EVERYTHING CHEESE PUFFS (GOUGÈRES)

Gougères (known less romantically as cheese puffs) are basically cheesy profiteroles. Traditionally, they are an accompaniment to wine tastings in their native Burgundy, which makes them a fitting addition to a booze-soaked Christmas party.

SERVES 8

175ml (¾ cup) whole (full-fat) milk

75ml (⅓ cup) water

115g (½ cup) unsalted butter, cubed

½ tsp fine sea salt

180g (1⅓ cups) plain (all-purpose) flour

6 large eggs, at room temperature: 5 whisked; 1 reserved

15g (¼ cup) Parmesan, finely grated

20g (3 tbsp) Gruyère cheese, finely grated

Everything Bagel Seasoning:

2 tsp poppy seeds

1 tbsp white sesame seeds

1 tbsp black sesame seeds

4 tsp dried onion flakes

2 tsp flaked salt

Filling:

225g (1 cup) cream cheese, softened

200ml (generous ¾ cup) double or whipping (heavy) cream

180g (1 cup) smoked salmon, finely chopped

20g (½ cup) finely chopped fresh chives

zest of 1 lemon

2 tsp lemon juice

salt and freshly ground black pepper, to taste

1. Preheat the oven to 220ºC/425ºF/gas 7 and line a baking tray with baking paper.

2. Combine the milk, water, butter and salt in a large saucepan and bring to the boil over a medium-high heat, stirring constantly. Add the flour and stir until a dough forms. Reduce the heat to medium and cook for about 2 minutes, stirring constantly with a wooden spoon, until the dough is slightly dried out.

3. Transfer to a food processor and pulse a few times to cool the dough slightly, then add the 5 whisked eggs and pulse until combined. Pulse in the cheeses.

4. Transfer the dough to a piping bag fitted with a plain 1cm (½in) nozzle. Pipe small mounds of dough, about 3cm (1in) in diameter, onto the lined baking tray.

5. Whisk the remaining egg with 1 tsp water to make an egg wash. In a separate bowl, mix together all the Everything Bagel Seasoning ingredients.

6. Brush the piped mounds with egg wash and sprinkle the tops generously with the seasoning.

7. Place the tray in the oven and immediately reduce the temperature to 180ºC/350ºF/gas 4. Bake the gougères for about 25–30 minutes until golden brown. Transfer to a wire rack to cool completely.

8. Meanwhile, whip together the cream cheese and cream in a bowl, until light and airy. Fold through the remaining filling ingredients, then transfer to a piping bag fitted with a large star-shaped nozzle.

9. Cut the top off each of the gougères with a serrated knife, then pipe the filling into the middle and rest the caps back on top.

INGRE

DIENTS

HUNTING FOR THE
threads of god

SU FILINDEU, WHICH LITERALLY TRANSLATES AS THE 'THREADS OF GOD', IS UNLIKE ANY OF THE DRIED PASTA SHAPES YOU MIGHT FIND SHRIVELLED ON THE SHELF OF YOUR LOCAL SUPERMARKET. MICROSCOPIC GOSSAMER FILAMENTS, HALF THE WIDTH OF ANGEL HAIR, ARE INTERWOVEN IN WHAT LOOKS MORE LIKE A FROZEN SPIDER'S WEB THAN FOOD.

For 300 years, female members of a single family have handed down the recipe, to the point where today there are only a handful of people left who are still capable of making the dish. As delicious as it is elusive, *su filindeu* is famous for being the rarest pasta in the world.

So special is this ingredient that twice a year, on the island of Sardinia, hungry pilgrims undertake a unique 20-mile trek to try it for themselves. Starting from the ancient city of Nuoro, their route winds through the rocky crags and parched fields that carpet the looming Mount Ortobene, towards the hallowed grounds of the Santuario di San Francesco church. In May and October, thousands brave the climb towards the sanctuary to celebrate the Feast of San Francesco and get their hands on a bowl of pasta.

On paper, the dish that motivates their efforts sounds deceptively simple. Semolina durum wheat, water and salt are mixed to make a rudimentary dough that must be carefully kneaded until it reaches the consistency of modelling clay, before being worked into individual rounded strands. These are stretched and folded over eight successive cycles, until 256 delicate fibres of pasta remain. With great care, the strings must then be laid across a custom-made wooden frame, criss-crossing three threaded layers over one another, creating a circular, luminous membrane. After drying in the sun for several hours, the crisp, wafer-thin sheets are crushed and laid in the bottom of a bowl, before being drowned in a hearty sheep's broth and covered in local Pecorino cheese. Mastering the entire method can take years.

Many outsiders have tried to tackle the 'threads of God'. Celebrity chefs have spent fruitless hours alongside the few women who have perfected the dish, attempting to conquer the endless rounds of weaving. In fact, almost every external effort to learn the art of *su filindeu* has been frustrated by failure.

Pasta might be most famous for its popular appeal, but as *su filindeu* proves, this ingredient can still be as mysterious as anything else on the table.

Haunted pasta factory

Be gone, long, moribund jokes about ghosts enjoying bowls of spook-hetti! The veil between the dead, the living and their dinner was lifted at what was one of America's most haunted buildings, the infamous Spaghetti Warehouse in downtown Houston. Pasta-obsessed spirits manifested themselves in various forms, including a long-dead train conductor, a man who fell down a lift shaft and a small girl holding a balloon. Think of these restless spirits next time you tuck into your favourite pastARGGGGH.

SPAGHETTI TREE HOAX

The British have always been a gullible bunch. On April 1st 1957, the BBC aired an infamous segment on the 'Great Swiss-Italian Spaghetti Harvest'. The three-minute clip featured hardy spaghetti farmers picking individual pasta strands from a tree, and convinced millions of viewers that their favourite Italian food was in fact not made, but grown. When baffled Brits demanded to know how they could grow their own pasta trees, the venerable broadcaster reportedly told them to 'place a sprig of spaghetti in a tin of tomato sauce and hope for the best'.

CREAMY CHICKEN FAJITA PENNE

This love-child of Tex Mex and Italian cuisine is a Twisted classic. There's something incredibly comforting about this combination of ingredients, an intricate alchemy of cheese, spice and pasta that is universally appealing and infinitely greater than the sum of its parts.

SERVES 4–6

3 medium chicken breasts

2 tbsp mild olive oil

1 tbsp unsalted butter

1 red onion, thinly sliced

3 mixed peppers, sliced

3 garlic cloves, crushed

1 tbsp tomato purée (paste)

3 tbsp fajita seasoning

400g (14oz) mixed tomatoes, roughly chopped

100ml (generous ⅓ cup) chicken stock

400ml (1¾ cups) double (heavy) cream

100g (generous 1 cup) Red Leicester or Cheddar, grated, plus extra to serve

400g (14oz) dried penne

salt and freshly ground black pepper, to taste

1. Season the chicken liberally with salt and pepper. Heat the oil in a heavy sauté pan over a medium heat, then fry the chicken breasts for around 5 minutes on each side, or until a deep golden brown (transfer to a hot oven to cook through if necessary). Set aside to cool, then tear into penne-sized shreds.

2. Add the butter to the same pan and fry the onion and peppers until soft and slightly charred in places, about 10 minutes. Add the garlic and fry until fragrant, then add the tomato purée and fajita seasoning. Fry for 1 minute, then add the tomatoes and reduce for a few more minutes until thick.

3. Pour in the stock and cream, bring to a gentle simmer and allow the sauce to thicken a bit more. Remove from the heat and leave to cool (if it's too hot, the cheese might split in the next step).

4. Stir through the cheese and return the shredded chicken to the pan.

5. Meanwhile, cook the pasta in plenty of salted boiling water until al dente, according to the packet instructions. Drain, then toss through the sauce, loosening with a little reserved pasta water if necessary.

6. Serve with lots of extra grated cheese, fajita-style.

BAKED JALAPEÑO POPPER CHICKEN SPAGHETTI

As ever with pasta 'al forno', the crust here is the best bit. Imagine the rich, spicy creaminess of a jalapeño popper weaved through masses of spaghetti. Make this and you won't have to!

SERVES 4–6

200g (2¼ cups) sharp
Cheddar, grated

200g (1¾ cups) low-moisture (aged)
mozzarella, grated

50g (¾ cup) Parmesan, finely grated

1½ tbsp cornflour (cornstarch)

1 tbsp olive oil

8 thick rashers smoked streaky
bacon, diced

2 fat garlic cloves, thinly sliced

200ml (generous ¾ cup) chicken stock

2–4 jalapeños, chopped

200ml (generous ¾ cup)
double (heavy) cream

120g (½ cup) cream cheese

½ roast chicken or 3 cooked chicken
breasts, shredded

1 tsp freshly ground black pepper

400g (14oz) spaghetti

salt, to taste

1. Preheat the oven to 180°C/350°F/gas 4.

2. Add all the cheeses to a bowl and toss with the cornflour until well covered. Set aside. eat.

3. Heat the olive oil in an ovenproof sauté pan over a medium heat and fry the bacon until the fat has rendered and it is quite crisp. Throw in the garlic and cook until sticky (but not browned), then drain any excess fat from the pan and return it to the heat. Add the chicken stock and jalapeños and cook until reduced by half, about 5 minutes. Add the cream, cream cheese, shredded chicken and black pepper, then add salt to taste (watch out for the saltiness of your bacon and stock). Bring up to a simmer, then remove from the heat.

4. Cook the spaghetti in plenty of well salted boiling water for 6 minutes, or very al dente, then transfer it to the sauce along with about 200ml (generous ¾ cup) pasta cooking water and half of the cheese mixture. Stir the cheese through the pasta and sauce to distribute – it should look quite wet at this stage. Sprinkle the remaining cheese mixture over the top of the spaghetti and bake in the oven for 15 minutes, uncovered.

5. Meanwhile, preheat the grill (broiler) to high.

6. Transfer the pan to the grill for a final few minutes, or until it has a rich golden crust on top. Let sit for a few minutes, then serve!

WELSH RAREBIT MAC 'N' CHEESE

The word 'rarebit' is apparently a corruption of 'rabbit'. Historically, people would mock the Welsh for being a bit stingy and so to serve someone 'Welsh rabbit' was to give them something inferior or ersatz. Likewise, a 'Welsh pearl' was of bad quality and a 'Welsh comb' was to brush your hair with your fingers. Harsh – and unfair, since Welsh rarebit is great.

SERVES 4–6

100g (scant ½ cup) unsalted butter, plus 3 tbsp melted

4 medium leeks, washed, trimmed and thinly sliced

150ml (⅔ cup) blonde beer

170g (6oz) sourdough bread, torn into small chunks

40g (generous ¼ cup) plain (all-purpose) flour

500ml (generous 2 cups) whole (full-fat) milk

1 tbsp Worcestershire sauce (or Henderson's relish, if you're veggie)

1 tbsp English mustard

½ tsp cayenne pepper

400g (14oz) good-quality dried elbow macaroni

400g (4½ cups) really nice mature Cheddar, grated

salt and freshly ground black pepper, to taste

1. Preheat the oven to 170°C/340°F/gas 4 and grease a large baking dish.

2. Heat half of the unsalted butter in a saucepan set over a low heat and gently fry the leeks for 30–40 minutes until you have a lightly caramelised tangle. Increase the heat, add the beer and let it reduce until almost completely evaporated. Set aside.

3. Toss the sourdough chunks in the melted butter, spread over a baking tray and toast in the oven for about 10 minutes until golden but not too dark (they get cooked again later).

4. In a large, heavy saucepan, heat the remaining butter until it foams, then add the flour and stir vigorously to make a smooth paste. Gradually beat in the milk with a wooden spoon, then stir in the Worcestershire sauce, mustard and cayenne pepper. Leave to bubble and thicken for 3–4 minutes. Stir in the leeks, then remove from the heat and let cool for 5 minutes.

5. Meanwhile, cook the macaroni in plenty of salted boiling water until al dente, according to the packet instructions. Drain, reserving a cup of pasta cooking water.

6. Add the pasta to the sauce, then add the Cheddar, a handful at a time, stirring as you go. Splash in a little pasta water if the sauce looks too thick. Season with salt and pepper, to taste.

7. Pour the mixture into the baking dish and top with the sourdough croutons. Bake for 20–25 minutes until golden and bubbling.

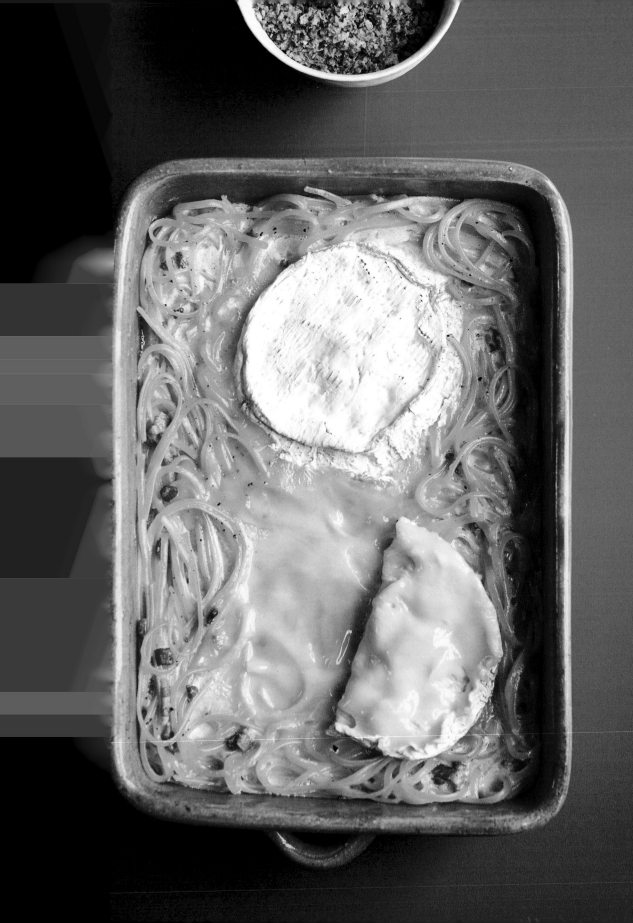

UPSIDE-DOWN CAMEMBERT LINGUINE

We all have those days where we throw caution to the wind and really treat ourselves. Next time the mood takes you and you're at a loss for what to eat, this outrageous recipe could be just the ticket – a decadent food sonnet to that comforting wheel of ooze, Camembert.

SERVES 4–6

1 tbsp olive oil

8 rashers streaky bacon, cut into strips

3 garlic cloves, crushed

150ml (⅔ cup) dry white wine

200ml (generous ¾ cup) chicken stock

300ml (1¼ cups) double (heavy) cream

70g (1 cup) Parmesan, grated

1 tbsp freshly ground black pepper

400g (14oz) dried linguine

1 x 250g (9oz) Camembert

salt, to taste

Crumb topping:

50g (3½ tbsp) unsalted butter

1 garlic clove, crushed

80g (2 cups) panko breadcrumbs

3 tbsp thyme leaves

20g (⅓ cup) Parmesan, finely grated

1. Preheat the oven to 180°C/350°F/gas 4.

2. Heat the olive oil in a large, heavy sauté pan over a medium heat. Fry the bacon until crispy, about 5 minutes, then add the garlic and cook for about 30 seconds until fragrant. Pour in the white wine and cook for about 2 minutes, allowing the alcohol to evaporate, then add the stock and bring up to a simmer. Add the cream, Parmesan and pepper, then season with salt to taste.

3. Meanwhile, cook the pasta in plenty of salted boiling water until very al dente, just less than it states on the packet instructions (it'll keep cooking in the oven). Drain and add to the pan with the sauce, toss well, then pour into a deep baking dish.

4. Split the Camembert horizontally into two halves and place them, cut-side down, on top of the pasta.

5. Bake for 10–15 minutes, or until the cheese has fully melted down into the pasta.

6. To make the crumb topping, melt the butter in a saucepan, add the garlic and fry until fragrant. Add the breadcrumbs and toast until light brown, then scatter in the thyme and Parmesan and continue stirring for another minute or so. Transfer to a bowl.

7. Peel off the Camembert skins and theatrically swirl the molten cheese through the pasta. Divide between bowls and shower with the toasted crumbs. Eat immediately.

SAUSAGE RIGATONI ALLA VODKA

Italian-American restaurants are probably not worth their salt if they don't feature a pasta 'alla vodka', a dish that shot to popularity in the 1970s following a regional Italian cooking competition. Essentially a creamy, spicy tomato sauce, the vodka ostensibly 'lifts' the spirit of the sauce. The Italians have been cooking with grappa (a brandy made from the pomace, or leftovers, of the winemaking process) for centuries, and some claim that this is where the origins of the dish really lie. So, if you have some grappa knocking about, use that instead.

SERVES 4–6

2 tbsp olive oil

6 good-quality sausages, casings removed

1 red onion, finely chopped

2 x 400g (14oz) cans whole plum tomatoes

2 garlic cloves, thinly sliced

1 tsp chilli flakes, or to taste

125ml (½ cup) vodka (or grappa if you're feeling posh)

50g (3½ tbsp) unsalted butter

1 tsp sugar

100ml (generous ⅓ cup) double (heavy) cream

½ nutmeg, finely grated

50g (¾ cup) Parmesan, finely grated, plus extra to serve

500g (1lb 2oz) dried short rigatoni or other tubular pasta

a good handful of basil leaves

salt and freshly ground black pepper, to taste

1. Heat the olive oil in a large stovetop casserole over a medium-high heat. Crumble in the sausagemeat and cook until well browned, about 5 minutes, breaking it up as you go. When there is a good amount of stickiness at the bottom of the pot, add the onion and a small pinch of salt. Reduce the heat and cook, stirring occasionally, until the onions are sweet and translucent, about 10 minutes. The moisture from the onion should deglaze some of the stickiness, but if at any point you see it catching, add a few tbsp water and crack on as before.

2. Meanwhile, drain 1 can of tomatoes and put the tomatoes into a bowl along with the second (undrained) can and crush them roughly by hand.

3. Add the garlic and chilli flakes to the pot and cook for a further few minutes, until the garlic smells good and is sticky, then add the crushed tomatoes, vodka or grappa, butter, sugar and another good pinch of salt. Rinse the tomato cans with a little water and add to the pot. Reduce the heat and cook for 1 hour, stirring occasionally, until the sauce is reduced, thick and delicious.

4. Add the cream and nutmeg to the sauce and bring back to a simmer for a few minutes, then remove from the heat and beat in the Parmesan. Check the seasoning – it should be very tasty. If not, add more salt.

5. Meanwhile, cook the pasta in plenty of salted boiling water according to the packet instructions, then drain reserving a little of the cooking water.

6. Add the pasta to the sauce and loosen with a splash of the reserved pasta water. Toss well, adding the basil at the very last. Serve with more Parmesan at the table.

KING PRAWN & LEMON FETTUCCINE ALFREDO

Try and find some nice big prawns (jumbo shrimp) for this. You may have noticed by now that we have a thing for creamy pasta; rest assured that the lemon lends this the perfect amount of zinginess, to lighten things up a bit.

SERVES 4–6

1 tbsp olive oil

2 tbsp unsalted butter

450g (1lb) king prawns (jumbo shrimp), shelled and deveined

1 shallot, finely chopped

2 garlic cloves, finely chopped

2 lemons: zest and juice of 1 lemon; 1 cut into wedges

500ml (generous 2 cups) double (heavy) cream

100g (1½ cups) Parmesan, finely grated

450g (1lb) dried fettuccine

2 tbsp chopped flat-leaf parsley, plus extra to serve

salt and freshly ground black pepper, to taste

1. Heat the oil and 1 tbsp of the butter in a large sauté pan over a medium–high heat. Season the prawns with salt and pepper, then sear on both sides until almost cooked through. Remove and set aside.

2. Add the remaining butter to the same pan and reduce the heat. Add the shallot and cook for about 5 minutes until soft and translucent, then add the garlic and cook until fragrant, about 1 minute. Add the lemon juice and reduce briefly, then add the cream, lemon zest and Parmesan and stir to combine. Gently simmer for 5 minutes or so until the sauce has thickened and coats the back of a spoon. Season with salt, pepper and more lemon juice to taste. It should be rich and creamy, yet bright with lemon.

3. Meanwhile, cook the fettuccine in plenty of salted boiling water until al dente, according to the packet instructions. Drain, reserving a cup of pasta cooking water.

4. Add the pasta to the sauce along with the prawns and chopped parsley. Toss well, adding a little pasta water to loosen.

5. Serve with extra parsley, black pepper and some lemon wedges at the table.

SPICED SLOW-COOKED BEEF SHIN PAPPARDELLE

The Venetians have been putting spices in their food since the Byzantine era, so this isn't actually too mental, although the numbing peppercorns aren't trad. Basically this is like Chinese dan dan noodles. It is worth nipping to a good butcher for the meat.

SERVES 4–6

2kg (4lb 6oz) bone-in beef shin, cut into large pieces, trimmed

2 tbsp oil

75g (⅓ cup) unsalted butter

1 large onion, finely chopped

2 small carrots, finely chopped

2 celery sticks, finely chopped

4 garlic cloves, finely chopped

2 fresh bay leaves

1 cinnamon stick

2 star anise

1 tbsp fennel seeds

4 tbsp tomato purée (paste)

½ x 750ml (25fl oz) bottle nice red wine

650ml (2¾ cups) beef stock

½ nutmeg, grated

500g (1lb 2oz) dried pappardelle

100g (1½ cups) Parmesan, finely grated

1–2 tbsp Sichuan peppercorns, toasted and ground, to serve

salt and freshly ground black pepper, to taste

1. Preheat the oven to 150°C/300°F/gas 2.

2. Season the beef shin liberally with salt and pepper on all sides. Set a large casserole or heavy ovenproof saucepan over a medium heat and add the oil. Working in batches, brown the beef thoroughly on all sides (don't rush this bit), then remove and set aside.

3. Reduce the heat and add 2 tbsp of the butter to the pot along with the onion, carrots, celery, garlic, bay and all the whole spices (apart from the nutmeg). Cook for at least 30 minutes until the vegetables are very soft, sweet and aromatic. As they are cooking, scrape to release any beef bits that have collected at the bottom of the pot – this is all good flavour.

4. Add the tomato purée and cook out for a couple of minutes, or until the oil starts to separate. Increase the heat, pour in the wine and cook until almost completely evaporated, about 10 minutes. Add the stock and bring to a light simmer, then tuck the beef pieces back into the pot, ensuring they are submerged in the liquid as much as possible. Cover with a damp circle of greaseproof paper, put the lid on and place in the oven. Cook for 5–6 hours, checking and turning the beef occasionally, until the meat has fallen from the bones and shreds easily with a fork.

5. Remove the meat and bones to a board and shred with two forks. Release any marrow from the bones, keeping it separate, then discard the bones (or reserve for a statement garnish).

6. If excessive, skim some fat from the residual sauce, then spoon in the marrow. Add the nutmeg and taste for salt and pepper. It should taste ridiculously good. Return the shredded meat to the sauce and bring back up to heat.

7. Meanwhile, cook the pasta in plenty of well salted boiling water until al dente, according to the packet instructions. Drain, reserving a cup of pasta cooking water.

8. Add the pasta, remaining butter and half of the Parmesan to the sauce and toss together to coat, adding a little pasta water to aid the process. The ragu should adhere to the pasta and be nice and glossy.

9. Arrange the pasta on a large platter (with bones to decorate, if you fancy) and finish with lots more Parmesan and a good dusting of the Sichuan pepper. Serve more of both at the table.

SICILIAN BRUSCHETTA PASTA SALAD

This pasta salad was inspired by pesto Trapanese, the Sicilian version of the famous Genoese classic. Usually made from almonds and raw tomatoes, we've included mint and pistachios too (all very Sicilian). The aim was to make this look like a massive flying bruschetta. As the photo suggests, we are extremely pleased with the result.

SERVES 6–8

600g (1lb 5oz) mixed tomatoes, chopped or halved if small

500g (1lb 2oz) dried fusilli

1 small red onion, very finely chopped

salt and freshly ground black pepper, to taste

Pesto:

100g (¾ cup) roasted shelled pistachios or toasted blanched almonds (or a mixture)

60g (2 cups) basil leaves, roughly chopped, plus a few sprigs for garnish

20g (⅔ cup) mint leaves, roughly chopped, plus a few sprigs for garnish

2 garlic cloves, crushed to a paste

150ml (⅔ cup) nice olive oil, plus extra to loosen

80g (1¼ cups) Parmesan, finely grated

1 small ice cube (optional)

salt, to taste

Bruschetta toasts:

sourdough bread, sliced

½ garlic clove, for rubbing

nice olive oil, for drizzling

flaked sea salt, for sprinkling

1. Season the tomatoes well with salt, then place in a large sieve or colander, cover loosely with clingfilm (plastic wrap) and set over a large bowl (big enough to take all of your cooked pasta) to drain for at least 1 hour.

2. Meanwhile, get on with your pesto. If using a pestle and mortar, bash and massage the nuts until you have a rough paste, then transfer to a bowl. Adding it gradually, grind the basil and mint to a fine green sludge, then add the garlic paste and loosen with most of the olive oil. Tip this mixture into the bowl with the nut paste and stir through the cheese and the remaining olive oil. Taste for salt and set aside. If using a food processor or blender, add the herbs, olive oil, nuts, garlic and the ice cube and process until you have a rough but homogeneous paste, then transfer to a bowl and stir through the cheese. Taste for salt and set aside.

3. Cook the pasta in plenty of salted boiling water according to the packet instructions until al dente, then drain and add to the bowl under the tomatoes (you won't need any pasta water). Toss the pasta through the tomato nectar – it will be absorbed by the hot pasta as it cools. When just a little warm, add three-quarters of the pesto and beat well to incorporate. You should have a wonderful thick sauce that just clings to your pasta. Transfer the pasta to a large serving platter.

4. Add the red onion to the tomatoes along with lots of black pepper and dress with a little olive oil. Arrange this mixture in the middle of the pasta, then blob the remaining pesto in and around the sea of tomatoes. Garnish with a few whole herbs, if you like.

5. For your bruschetta toasts, grill the slices of sourdough (a cast-iron griddle is good for this) until nicely charred, then rub with the halved garlic clove, drizzle with a little olive oil and sprinkle with some flaked salt. Arrange around your platter and serve, preferably in the garden on a hot day.

WRAPS

THAT'S
A Wrap

THE YEAR WAS 1982, THE COMPUTER HAD JUST BEEN VOTED THE 'TIME' MAN OF THE YEAR. MICHAEL JACKSON WAS ABOUT TO RELEASE THE GREATEST POP MUSIC ALBUM OF ALL TIME.

Vol au vents were the undisputed Christmas canapé of choice. And, in a quiet corner of Stamford, Connecticut, an unassuming ex-baseball pro was preparing to make fast food history.

Bobby Valentine is probably best known as the disastrous former coach of the world-famous Boston Red Sox. However, despite this unfortunate accolade, Valentine's greatest contribution to modern culture can only be fully appreciated if you look at his career beyond the ballpark. Apart from being a distinctly average baseball coach, Valentine was first and foremost a serious food enthusiast. Retiring as a player at the age of 29, he supplemented his income with an ongoing investment in the restaurant industry, owning and operating Bobby Valentine's Sports Gallery Cafe since 1980.

On one occasion in 1982, the famously spendthrift Valentine and his team were ambushed by the arrival of an erstwhile Sports Gallery investor. As fate would have it, this just happened to be the day after Valentine had decided to throw out his broken toaster and loudly declare to the staff that he had no intention of replacing it. Naturally, their guest then proceeded to request the only toasted thing on the menu – a club sandwich.

With the kitchen panicking at the prospect of an irate investor, Valentine seized the initiative. In a moment of inspiration he tore open a packet of tortillas, stuffed the ingredients for the club inside the soft floury shell, bundled the whole parcel into a cylinder, and sealed the contents with melted cheese. He didn't know it at the time, but Valentine had accidentally created an icon.

The hungry banker couldn't get enough. Before long, 'Club Sandwich Wraps' were a fixture of the Sports Gallery Cafe menu. Valentine's ingenious decision to pack traditionally American ingredients into a typically Mexican menu item struck a chord with everyone who ate it. Soon, the entire food industry was swimming in a sea of cornflour and filling.

It's not often that an ingredient lends itself to almost every food under the sun. If, like Valentine, you find yourself having to think on your feet, history tells you that you will always have one ally in the cupboard. As a blank canvas for different food thinking, you can't go wrong with a wrap.

MEXICAN *MOLDES*

In Guanajuato, in the vast, semi-arid region of the Central Mexican Plateau, the ancient tradition of decorating tortillas is upheld to this day by the indigenous Otomi population. For centuries, ornate images have been engraved into mesquite logs and natural dyes extracted from the local fauna, all in preparation for the 'stamping' of freshly made flour or corn tortillas.

Historically, these (completely edible) works of art were decorated with the faces of Saints, but now more commonly feature imagery from the surrounding landscape. Frequently offered to revered guests as a sign of respect, the carved mesquite *moldes* are still made and sold at local Bajio markets.

A few tortilla crafts

EYE MASK

JACK O' LANTERN

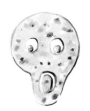

THE SCREAM

CROWN

MITRE

BOOK

CRANE

THE MOON

SHEET PAN CHICKEN FAJITA CRUNCHWRAP

This is the star of one of our biggest videos to date, and is an excellent twist for fajita night. We serve this with a little sour cream for dipping, which we'd highly recommend.

SERVES 8

4 chicken breasts
(about 600g/1lb 5oz), sliced

6 mixed peppers, sliced

3 red onions, sliced

3 tbsp olive oil

3 tbsp fajita seasoning

2 tbsp unsalted butter, melted

9 large flour tortillas

280g (3 cups) Cheddar, grated

400g (14oz) spicy tortilla chips

salt, to taste

1. Preheat the oven the 200°C/400°F/gas 6.

2. Pop the chicken, peppers and onions into a large roasting tray and dress with the oil, fajita seasoning and a good pinch of salt. Toss to ensure everything is well coated. Roast for 25 minutes, stirring occasionally, until the chicken is cooked through and everything is starting to take on some colour. Remove and set aside.

3. Brush the bottom of a large, non-stick baking tray with the melted butter. Lay 7 tortillas around the tray to cover, overlapping them as you go and leaving no gaps. Top the tortillas with half of the grated cheese, half of the chicken mixture and all of the tortilla chips, then top with the remaining chicken mixture and cheese. Cover the middle with the remaining tortillas and fold over the tortillas around the sides to make a giant parcel. Lay a sheet of greaseproof paper over the top, cover with another heavy baking tray and weigh down if necessary.

4. Turn the oven down to 180°C/350°F/gas 4 and bake for 30 minutes.

5. Remove the tray and weight and the greaseproof paper. If necessary, invert the crunchwrap parcel and grill (broil) for additional colour.

6. Tip the crunchwrap out onto a board, cut up and destroy!

CRISPY HOISIN DUCK CHIMICHANGAS

A chimichanga is basically a deep-fried burrito. Stuffed with crispy shredded hoisin duck, this is like a duck spring roll on heat.

SERVES 6

4 duck legs

¼ cinnamon stick

1 tsp fennel seeds

1 tsp black peppercorns

1 tbsp sesame oil

1 small carrot, peeled and julienned

¼ head of Chinese cabbage, shredded

2 spring onions (scallions), julienned, plus extra to serve

1 tsp finely chopped garlic

1 tsp finely chopped fresh root ginger

3 tbsp hoisin sauce, plus extra to serve

2 tbsp water

2½ tbsp plain (all-purpose) flour

6–8 large flour tortillas

salt, to taste

neutral oil, for shallow frying

cucumber, sliced into matchsticks, to serve

1. Pat the duck legs dry with kitchen paper, season well on both sides with salt and let sit at room temperature for 1½ hours.

2. Meanwhile, grind the cinnamon stick, fennel seeds and black peppercorns to a coarse powder in a pestle and mortar.

3. Preheat the oven to 150°C/300°F/gas 2.

4. Pat the duck legs dry again, then rub all over with the spice mixture. Place on a rack set over a baking tray, skin-side up, and roast for 1 hour 20 minutes.

5. Meanwhile, heat the sesame oil in a pan over a medium heat and fry the carrot and cabbage along with a pinch of salt for 2–3 minutes until wilted but still a little crunchy. Set aside.

6. Increase the oven temperature to 220°C/425°F/gas 7 and give the duck a final 10 minutes to really crisp up. Set aside to rest and cool, then pull the meat from the bones, skin and all, chop roughly, and transfer to a bowl to cool a little.

7. Stir the wilted vegetables, spring onions, garlic, ginger and hoisin sauce into the duck. The mixture shouldn't need salt if you've seasoned your vegetables and meat properly, but if you feel it needs it, go ahead.

8. Mix the flour with 2 tbsp water to form a paste. Using a finger, spread the flour paste across the top lip of one of the tortillas, then spoon a couple of large spoonfuls of the filling into the middle. Roll the tortilla up into a tight, fat cigar, folding in the sides as you go. Repeat to fill all the tortillas.

9. Heat a 3cm (1in) depth of oil in a deep heavy saucepan until very hot and fry your chimichangas until a rich brown on all sides. Remove with a slotted spoon to drain on kitchen paper. Serve with more hoisin sauce, spring onion and cucumber slices.

CHEESY JALAPEÑO CHICKEN ENCHILADAS

Jalapeños, those impeccably smooth, green and spicy torpedoes, have slid into many a Twisted recipe.

SERVES 6

85g (generous ⅓ cup) unsalted butter, plus extra for greasing

85g (scant ½ cup) plain (all-purpose) flour

530ml (2¼ cups) whole (full-fat) milk

530ml (2¼ cups) chicken stock

225g (1 cup) cream cheese

3 garlic cloves, crushed

a squeeze of lemon juice

6 thick rashers streaky bacon

450g (1lb) cooked chicken breast, shredded

7–8 jalapeños: 6 deseeded and diced; 1–2 cut into rings

200g (1¾ cups) low-moisture (aged) mozzarella, grated

10 x 20cm (8in) flour tortillas

salt and freshly ground black pepper, to taste

1. Preheat the oven to 180°C/350°F/gas 4. Grease a large baking dish.

2. Melt the butter in a saucepan over a medium heat, add the flour and cook, stirring, for 1 minute. Gradually add the milk and whisk until smooth, then whisk in the stock, cream cheese and garlic. Season with salt and pepper and a squeeze of fresh lemon and set aside.

3. Heat a dry frying pan (skillet) over a medium heat, and fry the bacon until crispy. Drain and let cool on kitchen paper, then chop into small pieces.

4. In a bowl, mix together the chicken, bacon, one-third of the cream sauce, the diced jalapeños and 150g (1¼ cups) of the mozzarella.

5. Fill each of the tortillas with the chicken mixture and roll into logs. Place them into the baking dish, brush with butter, and bake for 10 minutes until golden brown and just crispy.

6. Remove the dish from the oven and pour the remaining sauce over the top, spreading evenly. Sprinkle with the remaining grated cheese and the sliced jalapeños.

7. Bake for a further 10–15 minutes until bubbling and golden brown.

BUFFALO CHICKEN TRIANGLES

These are incredibly simple to make. Once you've got the hang of the little samosa-esque pouches, you can stuff them with just about anything that takes your fancy. This is one of our favourite fillings.

SERVES 6–8

300g (scant 1½ cups) cream cheese

100ml (½ cup) hot sauce
(we like Frank's)

75g (generous ¾ cup)
mature Cheddar, grated

50g (scant ½ cup) low-moisture
(aged) mozzarella, grated

1 tsp cayenne pepper

½ tsp garlic powder

1 tsp fine sea salt

3 tbsp finely chopped chives

3 cooked chicken breasts, shredded

3 tbsp plain (all-purpose) flour

3 tbsp water

10 flour tortillas, cut in half

neutral oil, for deep-frying

1. In a bowl, mix together the cream cheese, hot sauce, Cheddar, mozzarella, cayenne pepper, garlic powder, salt and chives to make a coarse paste, then fold in the shredded chicken.

2. Using a fork, whisk the flour and water together to make a smooth paste.

3. Take one of the tortilla halves and place it in front of you with the straight side furthest away from you. Brush the left-hand third of the tortilla's surface with the flour paste, then fold it around to the opposite side and press the two surfaces together to seal into a triangular pocket.

4. Carefully spoon some of the filling mixture into the pocket, leaving enough space to stick the top edges together. Brush these with the paste and firmly stick together to seal everything inside. Check for any gaps and, if necessary, seal with dabs of the paste.

5. Heat the oil in a deep, heavy saucepan to 175°C (350°F). Fry the triangles in batches of 3 or so (don't overcrowd the pan or the heat will drop too low and they won't cook properly – no thanks!). Remove with a slotted spoon to drain on kitchen paper, then transfer to a wire rack to cool slightly.

DIY PIZZA NACHOS

For those difficult days when you can't choose between pizza and nachos ... Choose pizza nachos. Choose life.

SERVES 6–8

60g (¼ cup) unsalted butter, melted

1 tsp garlic powder

1 tsp dried oregano

1 tsp dried basil

20g (¼ cup) Parmesan, grated

8 x 20cm (8in) flour tortillas, each cut into 8 triangles

115g (½ cup) pizza sauce

115g (1 cup) pizza mozzarella, grated

70g (½ cup) mini pepperoni slices

1. Preheat the oven to 180°C/350°F/gas 4. Line a baking tray (or 2) with baking paper.

2. In a bowl, mix together the butter, garlic powder, herbs and Parmesan. Add the tortilla pieces and toss to coat evenly.

3. Arrange the coated tortilla pieces on the lined trays without overlapping. Bake for 8–10 minutes until crispy and just golden. Keep an eye on them as they can crisp quickly.

4. Layer the nachos in a roasting pan and top with the pizza sauce, mozzarella and pepperoni.

5. Bake for 8 minutes, or until the cheese has melted. Tuck in!

DEEP-DISH PIZZA CRUNCHWRAP

The lineage of this dish can be traced back to Italy, then over the Atlantic with the Italian immigrants to Chicago, where the Neapolitan original got a thicker crust and a huge pile of toppings on top of the mozzarella. We've taken the 'deep-dish' concept and proudly shoved it into a crunchwrap.

SERVES 6–8

2 tsp oil, or more if needed

650g (1lb 7oz) sausages, casings removed

250g (9oz) green peppers, diced

250g (9oz) mushrooms, sliced

1 medium onion, finely chopped

5 garlic cloves, minced

900g (4 cups) tomato passata

2 tsp dried oregano

1 tsp dried chilli flakes

2 tsp sugar

6 large flour tortillas

400g (14oz) mozzarella, sliced

140g (1 cup) pepperoni slices

20g (¼ cup) Parmesan, finely grated, to serve

salt and freshly ground black pepper, to taste

1. Preheat the oven to 180°C/350°F/gas 4.

2. Heat the oil in a large sauté pan over a medium-high heat. Add the sausagemeat, breaking it up with a wooden spoon as you go, and cook for about 5 minutes, or until well browned. Remove with a slotted spoon to a large bowl.

3. In the same pan, cook the peppers and mushrooms for about 10 minutes until soft and caramelised, then remove to the bowl with the sausagemeat.

4. Add another glug of oil to the pan, if needed, and cook the onion for about 5 minutes, or until soft and translucent. Add the garlic and cook for 1 minute until aromatic. Add the passata, oregano and chilli flakes and bring to the boil, then reduce to a simmer and cook for about 15 minutes until thickened. Taste and season with the sugar and some salt and pepper – the sauce should be slightly sweet with a kick.

5. Add about 115g (½ cup) of the sauce to the sausage mixture in the bowl and stir to coat. Set the remaining sauce aside to cool.

6. Line a large ovenproof frying pan (skillet) or a deep round baking pan with baking paper, then lay 5 tortillas into the pan so that they cover the bottom and overlap. Place just over half of the mozzarella into the middle, followed by the sausage mixture. Arrange a layer of sliced pepperoni on top, then top with the remaining mozzarella. Place the final tortilla on top to cover, then fold over the edges of the tortillas to enclose. Place a piece of greaseproof paper on top, then weight down with another heavy flat-bottomed pan.

7. Bake for 25 minutes, then remove and turn the wrap over onto a board, then slide it back into the pan. Spread the top with a good layer of the tomato sauce and return to the oven for 5 minutes. Sprinkle with grated Parmesan before serving.

8. Serve with any remaining tomato sauce and extra Parmesan on the side.

SFC

(SCOTTISH FRIED CHICKEN)

AS WILL SURPRISE NO ONE WHO'S VISITED A GLASWEGIAN TAKEAWAY, SCOTLAND HAS ALWAYS TAKEN DEEP-FRYING EXTREMELY SERIOUSLY.

It takes a particular kind of cooking brain to come up with something as madcap as the deep-fried Mars bar. It therefore shouldn't come as any great surprise to learn that the world owes England's northern neighbour a considerable debt when it comes to fried chicken.

Before the Middle Ages, chicken and oil hardly mixed. In most of Europe, poultry was prepared in much the same way – either stuffed into a boiling pot or roasted over an open flame. Although this produced some decent results, not everyone was left satisfied. It took some misunderstood genius, sitting in a murky, medieval Scottish scullery, to decide to do things a little differently.

Whoever this forgotten Titan from cooking history was, he or she gave the world a completely new way to think about chicken. They realised that completely submerging a bird in boiling fat not only helped it remain moist and juicy, but also gave it a satisfying crunch unlike anything else on the menu. Deep-frying might have been done before, but no one had decided to give chicken the treatment. This was breaking new ground.

Despite this development, the food differed dramatically from how we might expect fried chicken to taste today. This was due in no small part to the cooks' laissez-faire attitude to the spice rack. The first fried chickens were unbattered, unseasoned and unrefined, with Scottish patrons apparently favouring birds that sat bubbling for a few minutes, before being served with as little alteration as possible.

It was not until the seventeenth and eighteenth centuries, when Scottish immigrants began to arrive in North America, that the method began to evolve. Enslaved Africans brought with them their own traditions, involving battering, seasoning and shallow-frying. It didn't take long for the two techniques to come together, and the rest is southern-fried history.

There are two lessons to learn from the story of fried chicken's Scottish origins. Firstly, not all the edible things to ever have come out of Britain are inherently horrible. Secondly, there's no telling where or when something delicious and chicken-y might pop up. Introduce this ingredient to almost any culture and you can quickly unlock a treasure trove of awesome things to eat. In the hands of the right cook, chicken makes everything better.

Famous chickens from history

250 BC

Anyone doubting the awesome power of the chicken is in dire need of a history lesson. In Ancient Rome, fortune tellers would use feeding chickens to determine the future, in a solemn ritual known as auspicium ex tripudiis. In 249 BC, Consul Publius Claudius Pulcher made the mistake of ignoring a bad chicken 'reading' and threw the offending sacred birds into the sea. His forces were promptly slaughtered by Carthaginians at the disastrous Battle of Drepana.

1945

Not only can chickens foretell impending doom, some may actually be immortal. In 1945, a Colorado cock known as 'Miracle Mike' became an international sensation after surviving his own execution. His would-be murderer and subsequent tour manager, Lloyd Olsen, left just enough of Mike's brain stem attached to his spine after a botched beheading to allow him to survive for 18 months after the event, appearing at a series of shows across America. Mike eventually passed away after accidentally choking on an over-sized piece of grain before a performance in Phoenix, Arizona.

1974

Not all heroes wear capes; some wear chicken costumes. Californian legend, Ted Giannoulas, has made his name by appearing at thousands of different sporting events during a 40-year career spent dressed as a giant chicken. Affectionately known as 'The Famous Chicken', 'The KGB Chicken' or just 'The Chicken', Giannoulas has attended more than 5,000 sporting events, famously stealing the show at Wrestlemania XV, and even recorded a cover of Rod Stewart's - 'Da Ya Think I'm Sexy?'.

REALLY GOOD FRIED CHICKEN SANDWICHES

If you're going to bother making fried chicken at home, you may as well do it properly. So many recipes out there are misleading, misinformed or crap. There is an amazing fried chicken shop in London called Butchies and this is basically how they do it (minus the industrial pressure fryer).

SERVES 6–8

8 good-quality, boneless skinless chicken thighs

1 x Cheat's Buttermilk Brine **(p.29)**

3 tbsp vodka

2 large eggs, beaten

200g (1½ cups) Italian '00' flour

100g (¾ cup) plain (all-purpose) flour

20g (3 tbsp) freshly ground black pepper

14g (1 level tbsp) fine sea salt

½ tsp garlic powder

1 tsp cayenne pepper

½ tsp paprika

rapeseed oil, for frying

To serve:

Potato Rolls **(p.20)**

Garlic & Herb Mayo **(p.25)**

Bread & Butter Pickles **(p.24)**

shredded iceberg lettuce

1. Submerge the chicken thighs in the buttermilk brine and refrigerate for 16–20 hours.

2. When you're ready to cook, bring the chicken out to come up to room temperature.

3. Meanwhile, beat the vodka into the eggs and place in a shallow bowl. In a shallow, 23cm (9in) wide baking dish, combine both flours with the black pepper, salt, garlic powder, cayenne pepper and paprika.

4. Remove the chicken thighs from the marinade and place on a wire rack to drip-dry completely. If they are still very wet, you can dab them a little with kitchen paper. Cover the thighs in the seasoned flour, ensuring it gets everywhere (all the nooks and crannies) and nothing is wet. Thoroughly shake off any excess and set them aside.

5. Drizzle 2 tbsp of the vodka/egg mixture into the remaining flour, then carefully and quickly distribute it through the flour with your fingertips (do not overwork it or you'll have a tough breading).

6. Lower a floured chicken thigh into the remaining vodka/egg mixture, turning it to coat thoroughly, then allow any excess to drip off before dropping it into the craggly breading mixture. Squeeze the breading firmly onto each side of the thigh, flipping a couple of times between squeezes, then carefully lift out onto a rack. Repeat with the others, then leave to rest for 15 minutes.

7. Fill a cast-iron skillet or a deep heavy saucepan with a 3cm (1in) depth of oil and heat to 180ºC/350ºF. Working in batches, lower the breaded thighs into the oil and fry for 6–7 minutes, turning them a couple of times to ensure even browning. Use a slotted spoon to transfer the cooked thighs to a rack to drain.

8. Toast the rolls (we like to brush them with butter and griddle them for a charred flavour), slather with mayonnaise, then load with the chicken thighs, pickles and lettuce.

HONEY-MUSTARD CHICKEN LOG

This is our favourite from a noble pantheon of viral-friendly 'logs'. This may look a little daunting to make, but it's actually really easy and one of the most impressive things you can proudly flourish at guests attending your next dinner party.

SERVES 6–8

2 tbsp unsalted butter

1 large brown onion, finely chopped

100g (1¾ cups) fresh white breadcrumbs

20g (½ cup) fresh thyme leaves

20g (½ cup) fresh sage leaves, finely chopped

9 pork sausages (at least 90% pork), casings removed

1 tsp fine sea salt

1 tsp black pepper

60g (¼ cup) wholegrain mustard

30g (2 tbsp) Dijon mustard

90g (5 tbsp) honey, plus extra as needed

1 garlic clove, crushed

6 large equal-sized chicken breasts

500g (1lb 2oz) thickly cut streaky bacon

400ml (1¾ cups) double (heavy) cream

lemon juice, to taste

salt and freshly ground black pepper, to taste

1. Preheat the oven to 180°C/350°F/gas 4.

2. Heat the butter in a heavy frying pan (skillet) over a medium heat until it foams, then add the onion and gently cook until soft, about 5 minutes. Set aside.

3. Combine the breadcrumbs, thyme, sage, sausagemeat, salt and pepper in a large bowl and use your hands to mix together. In a separate bowl, whisk together the mustards, honey and garlic. Season to taste and split into two bowls.

4. Butterfly the chicken breasts and use a rolling pin to individually bash them out to an even thickness. Arrange the flattened chicken on a large sheet of greaseproof paper to form a rectangular shape, ensuring that they are overlapping. Your rectangle should be 4 breasts long and 3 breasts high.

5. Brush the chicken square with one of the bowls of honey-mustard mixture. Use your hands to spread the stuffing mixture over the chicken, leaving around 3cm (1in) along the edge furthest from you free and around 1cm (½in) of the sides free. Pat the mixture down so it adheres to the chicken – this layer must not be too thick or it won't roll up easily.

6. Use the greaseproof paper to lift up the edge of the chicken closest to you and, very carefully and gently (yet tightly – nobody wants a floppy log!), roll the whole thing up, pulling the paper away as you go. Set the log on a baking tray in the freezer to firm the chicken up a bit.

7. To make the bacon weave, stretch out each rasher by gently but firmly scraping down the length of it with a knife. This prevents them shrinking too much when they cook. Lay half of them down next to each other in a line as long as your chicken log – they'll need to be long enough to wrap around the whole thing. Lift up alternate pieces of each row of bacon rashers and lay one piece horizontally along them to start the weave, then place the vertical pieces back down to cover. Lift up the other alternate vertical pieces and fold them back over the horizontal piece, then lay another piece of horizontal bacon over the vertical ones. Repeat until you have a woven bacon mat.

8. Take the chicken from the freezer and gently ease it onto one side of the bacon mat, then roll the whole thing up to form your impressive log. Bake in the middle of the oven for 40 minutes, then remove and brush with honey. Return to the oven for a final 20–30 minutes, or until the log is cooked through and the bacon is crisp.

9. Meanwhile, heat the remaining honey-mustard mixture in a small saucepan with the cream and simmer until the sauce coats the back of a spoon. Add salt, pepper and a squeeze of lemon, to taste. Serve alongside slices of the chicken log.

CHIP SHOP BATTERED CHICKEN SLIDERS

Why does fish get to have all the fun? This curry sauce is the real deal, and works really well with the maltiness of the batter.

SERVES 6–8

Curry sauce:

1 tbsp vegetable oil

1 tbsp unsalted butter

1 large onion, chopped

2 garlic cloves, finely chopped

1 tbsp mild curry powder

½ tsp Chinese five-spice

150g (1½ cups) apple, chopped

500ml (generous 2 cups) vegetable stock

1 tbsp cornflour (cornstarch), mixed with 2 tbsp stock

1 tbsp honey, or to taste

½ tsp celery salt, or to taste

a squeeze of lemon juice

salt, to taste

Chicken:

2 chicken breasts, butterflied and cut into 8–10 pieces

neutral oil, for deep-frying

200g (1½ cups) plain (all-purpose) flour

70g (¾ cup) cornflour (cornstarch)

1 tsp black pepper

1 heaped tsp baking powder

350ml (1½ cups) amber ale, very cold

fine sea salt, to taste

To serve:

Milk Buns **(p.22)**

Quick Pickled Onions **(p.23)**

salted butter, for spreading

1. For your curry sauce, heat the oil and butter in a large saucepan, add the onion and garlic with a pinch of salt and sweat for about 5 minutes until sweet and translucent. Add the spices, turn through the onions, then throw in the apple. Cook for a few minutes, until the apple is starting to break down a bit, then add the vegetable stock and simmer until reduced by half, 7–8 minutes.

2. Transfer the mixture to a food processor and blend until smooth, then return it to the pan. Over a low heat, whisk in the cornflour mixture to thicken a little, then finish with the honey, celery salt and a squeeze of lemon if you think it needs it. Keep warm.

3. Season your chicken lightly with salt and let sit at room temperature for 30 minutes. Meanwhile, heat the oil in a deep, heavy saucepan to 175ºC (350ºF).

4. Whisk together the flours, pepper and baking powder along with 1 tsp salt. Pat the chicken pieces dry with kitchen paper and dust each piece in the seasoned flour, shaking off the excess. Set aside.

5. Gently mix the beer into the remaining flour to make a batter. Dunk a floured chicken piece into the batter, ensuring it is evenly coated, then allow the excess to drip off a bit. Carefully lower into the hot oil and fry for about 4 minutes until a rich golden brown and very crisp. Fry no more than 3 or 4 pieces at a time, otherwise the temperature of the oil will drop and the batter will absorb too much oil and be soggy. Remove with a slotted spoon to briefly drain on kitchen paper, then transfer to a rack while you fry the rest.

6. Toast your milk buns and butter liberally. Load your chicken into the buns with the curry sauce and pickled onions. Dig in.

CHICKEN CAESAR SCHNITZEL SANDWICHES

Chicken schnitzel was delicious as it was, but this takes things to a whole new level. Serve these with lemon wedges and extra sauce, for dipping.

SERVES 4

6 slices of white bread, crusts removed

130g (1 cup) plain (all-purpose) flour

2 large eggs, beaten

1 tbsp Dijon mustard

20g (¼ cup) Parmesan, grated

1 tsp lemon zest

2 chicken breasts

vegetable oil, for shallow frying

salt and freshly ground black pepper, to taste

Caesar dressing:

6 anchovy fillets, packed in oil, drained

2 garlic cloves

1 large egg

2 tbsp Dijon mustard

juice of 1 lemon

20g (¼ cup) Parmesan, grated

235ml (1 cup) neutral oil

freshly ground black pepper, to taste

To serve:

½ white onion, thinly sliced

juice of 1 lemon

a handful of fresh parsley leaves, whole

1 head romaine lettuce, chopped

Potato Rolls **(p.20)**

Garlic Parsley Butter **(p.29)**

lemon wedges, to serve

1. Preheat the oven to 180°C/350°F/gas 4.

2. Meanwhile, put all of the dressing ingredients, except the oil, into a large cylindrical vessel, tall and wide enough for a hand-held stick (immersion) blender. Blend until the anchovies and garlic are completely smooth, then gradually stream in the oil as the blender is running and the dressing will thicken. Taste and season with black pepper, then chill in the refrigerator.

3. Break the bread into small bits, then spread over a baking tray and bake for about 8 minutes until dry and slightly golden. Let cool, then transfer to a food processor and blitz to a fine crumb.

4. Place the breadcrumbs, flour and eggs in separate shallow bowls. Season the flour with salt and pepper and whisk the Dijon mustard into the eggs. Mix the Parmesan and lemon zest into the breadcrumbs and season with salt and pepper.

5. Use a large sharp knife to cut each chicken breast in half horizontally, then place a chicken fillet between 2 sheets of clingfilm (plastic wrap). Use a meat mallet or a rolling pin to gently pound until thin. Repeat with the remaining fillets.

6. Dip the chicken fillets one at a time into the flour, shaking off any excess, then into the egg mixture, allowing the excess to drip back into the bowl, followed by the breadcrumbs, pressing gently to give a thorough coating. Set aside for 10 minutes.

7. Meanwhile, toss the onion in the lemon juice and set aside to macerate for 10 minutes or so (this will take the bit out of them).

8. Heat a 5mm (¼in) depth of oil in a heavy frying pan (skillet) and fry the chicken pieces until crispy and golden brown, 2–3 minutes per side. Remove with a slotted spoon to drain on a rack.

9. Squeeze the onion of any excess juice and transfer to a bowl with the romain lettuce and the whole parsley leaves. Toss with a few tablespoons of dressing. Slice the rolls in half and spread with garlic butter, then toast or griddle until golden brown. Spread each side with more of the dressing, then load with a piece of schnitzel and some of the dressed salad. Serve with additional lemon wedges on the side.

SKILLET CHICKEN TWO WAYS

The idea behind skillet chicken is that it only takes one pan and should be super-simple. For the Jalapeño Popper version we've gone for pickled jalapeños – firstly, because they're often easier to find than their fresh counterparts and secondly, we think that slight sharpness is vital in cutting through all the rich dairy. For the French Onion Chicken, the trick is simply to treat the onions with love, gently coaxing them to that magical caramelised state before melting them with cheese.

SERVES 3

For the French onion skillet chicken:

2 tbsp mild olive oil

3 chicken breasts

1 tbsp unsalted butter

4 large brown onions, sliced as thinly as possible

3½ tbsp Cognac

600ml (2½ cups) chicken stock (as good quality as possible)

3½ tbsp double (heavy) cream

100g (scant 1 cup) Gruyère cheese, grated

salt and freshly ground black pepper, to taste

For the jalapeño popper skillet chicken:

2 tbsp olive oil

3 chicken breasts

100g (3½oz) streaky bacon, chopped into thin strips

2 garlic cloves, minced

100g (3½oz) pickled jalapeños, finely diced

400ml (1¾ cups) double (heavy) cream

100g (scant ½ cup) cream cheese

200g (generous 1 cup) Cheddar, grated

salt and freshly ground black pepper, to taste

FRENCH ONION

1. Preheat the grill (broiler) to high.

2. Heat the skillet (or large, heavy frying pan) over a medium heat and add the oil. Season the chicken breasts well with salt and pepper, then fry until deeply golden on both sides and cooked through, about 10 minutes, then set aside somewhere warm.

3. Reduce the heat to the lowest you can go, add the butter to the pan, then add the onions and cook gently for around 1 hour, stirring all the time, until translucent and transformed into a sweet, golden nest. Pour in the Cognac and briefly cook off the alcohol, then add the chicken stock. Increase the heat slightly and cook until reduced to a thick gravy-like sauce, about 10 minutes.

4. Add the double cream, lots of black pepper and salt to taste, then return the chicken to the pan and heat through.

5. Sprinkle the chicken with cheese and place under the grill. Cook until melted.

6. Serve with buttery, mustardy, mashed potatoes.

JALAPEÑO POPPER

1. Heat the skillet (or large, heavy frying pan) over a medium heat and add the oil. Season the chicken breasts well with salt and pepper, then fry until deeply golden on both sides and cooked through, about 10 minutes, then set aside somewhere warm.

2. Reduce the heat and add the bacon to the skillet. Cook until crisp, about 5 minutes, then add the garlic and jalapeños and cook for about 1 minute until the garlic smells fragrant.

3. Pour over the double cream and allow to reduce slightly, then turn off the heat and allow the mixture to cool.

4. Fold in the cheeses and season to taste, then add the chicken breasts back to the pan and serve. This dish is delicious with fries.

FOIL-BALL ROAST CHICKEN

This really is an excellent way to roast a chicken. Salting the meat in advance makes the meat taste of so much more. You can be quite generous with the seasoning; the salt (along with the dry air from the fridge-chilling process) is key to that crispy skin. Keep the removed backbone and roast it alongside the chicken, then use for making stock.

SERVES 4

1 good-quality chicken
(about 1.6kg/3lb 8oz)

fine sea salt

groundnut, vegetable
or sunflower oil

1. Spatchcock your chicken, or ask your butcher to do it for you. Pat it dry with kitchen paper and liberally season with lots of fine sea salt all over, ensuring to get it into all the nooks and crannies. Lay the chicken on a baking tray and chill in the refrigerator, uncovered, for at least 24 hours (48 hours is best).

2. When you are ready to roast, bring the chicken out to come to room temperature and preheat the oven to full whack – 240°C/475°F/gas 9.

3. Pat the chicken dry with kitchen paper once again and rub all over with oil. Sprinkle with a little more salt.

4. Grab 2 individual sheets of foil and scrunch each up to roughly the size of a tennis ball. Place each ball under the bottom half of the chicken breasts (next to the legs). This should expose and tighten the skin that until now has been sheltered down by the thigh and will maximise the amount of crisp skin you will yield from your bird.

5. Place the chicken in the oven, legs-first, and roast for about 45 minutes, until evenly and richly golden, puffing in places and perhaps charring at the wing tip. If you're partial to an instant-read thermometer (and you should be, they're so useful), you want the temperature through the leg to be 85°C/185°F and 70°/158°F at the breast, or thereabouts. However, if it looks great and you can easily pinch the meat from the leg, it's done. Leave to rest for 15 minutes or so, then joint and use as you wish.

POTATOES

THE LOST LAND
of the potato

ON THE SURFACE, THERE ISN'T MUCH TO A POTATO. MUDDY BROWN CHILDHOOD MEMORIES OF BLAND JACKETS AND SOGGY WEDGES LEAVE TOO MANY OF US WITH THE FEELING THAT SPUDS ARE ACTUALLY PRETTY BORING.

Despite being eaten all over the world, there is only one country that really proves just how special this ingredient can be.

Peru isn't like most places you might associate with potatoes. Instead of flat green fields full of slowly sprouting tubers, the country is fractured into diverse, distinct habitats. On the coast, the sands of the Sechura Desert almost spill straight into the ocean, while the eastern border is overrun with lush, tropical jungle. Neither of these seem likely places to make chips. Yet, it is here that you will find more potato varieties than anywhere else on earth.

Home to an astonishing 4,000 unique subspecies, Peru produces potatoes of every possible shape and size. Local markets burst with produce painted into shades of yellow, red, purple and blue, with each strain bringing something new and exciting to the party. Some reveal concentric circles of colour as soon as they are cut in two, while others look like little more than mislaid gravel from a forgotten garden path. It's a far cry from sifting through knobbly dull lumps in the local supermarket.

Apart from the bombastic colours, what's most striking about Peruvian potatoes is how they feel and taste. The ordinarily subtle textural differences between waxy and floury give way to a cornucopia of stark contrasts, from crumbly to spongy, to stringy and everything in between.

A spectrum of sour, sweet and deeply savoury flavours mean that there's a Peruvian potato to suit every palate. You just need to know where to look.

Unfortunately, it's hugely impractical for most of us to hop on a flight to Peru for our weekly potato shop. However, there's no reason why the Peruvian respect for what the potato is and can be shouldn't translate into our kitchens. Andean farming is all about recognising the diversity of what you have to hand and celebrating it. As Peru proves, there's no excuse for dinner to be boring when there's a spud involved.

Potatoes around the house

Unless you live in Peru, potatoes aren't necessarily the sexiest of tubers. After spending the sixteenth century as the latest trendy foreign food thing, they have subsequently settled into the rather predictable routine of chips, crisps and mash. Look further than these humdrum applications however and a whole world of starch-based fun opens up. For example, you can use a potato to:

1. FIX A BROKEN WINDSCREEN WIPER

The cut side of a potato rubbed over a windscreen will coat the glass in starch – the water will then slide off, leaving the glass clear.

2. RELIEVE THE SYMPTOMS OF AN INSECT BITE

Simply slice in half and apply the cut side to the affected area. When the itching subsides, remove the potato and rinse with water.

3. CLEAN TARNISHED SILVER

Bathing precious family heirlooms in the water used to boil potatoes may seem weird, but it actually can get rid of any pesky patina marks.

TRIPLE-COOKED SPICY CAJUN FRIES

Proper chips, these. If you can't find beef dripping (seriously, who can?), parboiling your potatoes in stock is an inexpensive shortcut to massive flavour. It also makes the fries taste a bit like BBQ Beef Hula Hoops – the best flavour.

SERVES 6

1.2kg (2lb 10oz) large, floury potatoes (the bigger, the better)

2 tbsp fine sea salt

1.5l (6¼ cups) beef stock (from stock cubes), or enough to cover

neutral oil, for deep-frying

Cajun spice:

2 tsp fine sea salt

1½ tsp soft light brown sugar

1 tsp cayenne pepper, or to taste

2 tsp ground cumin

1 tbsp onion powder

1 tbsp garlic powder

1 tsp paprika

½ tsp smoked paprika

1. Peel your potatoes and cut into very fat, long fries, placing them to soak in a large bowl of cold water as you go. Rinse them in a few changes of water to get rid of the starch.

2. Place in a large saucepan with the salt and cover with beef stock. Bring to a light simmer and cook for about 15 minutes, or until your fries are about to fall apart, but not quite. Use a slotted spoon to lift them out onto a rack to completely steam dry.

3. Heat the oil in a deep, heavy saucepan to 140°C (285°F) (an instant-read kitchen thermometer is useful here) and use a slotted spoon or frying basket to lower in half of your cooled, dry fries. The temperature should drop to about 130°C (265°F). Try to maintain it around this point and cook the fries for 10 minutes or so until a crisp skin has formed but they are not yet browning. Lift the fries out onto the rack, then fry your second batch in the same way and remove.

4. Increase the heat of the oil to 180°C (350°F). Fry both batches separately for a further few minutes, or until they begin to float, at which point you know they're ready. Drain briefly on kitchen paper, then place in a large bowl.

5. Concoct your Cajun spice mix and cover your fries in it, tossing well to coat. Serve.

MASHED POTATO DIPPERS

If you're lucky enough to have leftover mash, this is the ultimate use for it. Stuff it full of fried bacon and Cheddar, cut it into discs and breadcrumb it. Being economical never looked so sexy.

SERVES 8

1.2kg (2lb 10oz) floury potatoes, peeled and diced (or about 1kg/2lb 3oz leftover mash)

12 bacon rashers, cooked until crisp

200g (generous 2 cups) Cheddar cheese, grated

10g (¼ cup) finely chopped chives

1 tsp fine sea salt

1 tsp freshly cracked black pepper

250g (1¼ cups) plain (all-purpose) flour

3 eggs, whisked

250g (3¼ cups) seasoned fine dried breadcrumbs

neutral oil, for frying

sour cream, to serve

1. If not using leftover mash, put the potatoes in large saucepan and cover with water. Bring to the boil and cook until tender to the point of a knife, 15–20 minutes. Drain and place back in the pan to steam dry. Mash until smooth or put the potatoes through a ricer into a large bowl and let cool completely.

2. Crumble the bacon into the mash, along with the cheese, chives, salt and pepper and mix to combine.

3. Spread the mash in a layer over a large baking tray lined with baking paper and press into an even layer. Chill in the refrigerator for 30 minutes –1 hour until firm.

4. Remove the mash from the fridge and use a 8cm (3in) round cookie cutter to cut it into discs. Roll up any remaining mash mix and continue to cut into discs until it is used up.

5. Place the flour, eggs and breadcrumbs into separate shallow bowls.

6. Coat each potato cake in flour, shaking off any excess, then dip each into the egg to coat, then into the seasoned breadcrumbs until well coated.

7. Heat a 1cm (½in) depth of oil in a deep heavy frying pan (skillet) and fry the potato cakes for 5–6 minutes, flipping halfway through, until crisp and golden brown. Remove to drain on kitchen paper.

8. Serve with sour cream. Enjoy!

LOADED FRIES TWO WAYS

Are there many sights more glorious than an enormous pile of fries? We don't think so. Particularly when topped with your favourite things: lasagne and BBQ chicken. These loaded fries might be best reserved for a special occasion (dog's birthday, break-up anniversary) with a fair few friends – they serve a lot of people and aren't exactly 'clean eating'.

SERVES 8

For the lasagne topped fries:

1 tbsp mild olive oil

200g (7oz) pancetta, cubed

1kg (2lb 3oz) minced (ground) beef (10% fat)

1 large brown onion, finely diced

3 garlic cloves, crushed

250g (generous 1 cup) passata

1 tbsp tomato purée (paste)

150ml (⅔ cup) red wine

150ml (⅔ cup) beef stock

100ml (generous ⅓ cup) double (heavy) cream

4 fresh lasagne sheets, chopped into small squares

40g (⅖ cup) Parmesan, grated, plus extra for sprinkling

2 x 125g (4½oz) fresh mozzarella balls, torn

1kg (2lb 3oz) frozen fries

salt, to taste

For the BBQ chicken loaded fries:

4 chicken breasts

400ml (1¾ cups) barbecue sauce

1kg (2lb 3oz) frozen fries

150g (generous 1½ cups) Cheddar, grated

200g (7oz) streaky bacon, cut into small strips and fried until crisp

3 tbsp pickled jalapeños, diced

salt and freshly ground black pepper, to taste

Sauce:

225g (1 cup) mayonnaise

110ml (scant ½ cup) sour cream

½ tsp paprika

½ tsp onion powder

¼ tsp garlic powder

1 tbsp dried chives

1 tbsp dried parsley

½ tsp fine sea salt

LASAGNE-TOPPED LOADED FRIES

1. Heat the oil in a large heavy sauté pan, add the pancetta and fry until nicely browned and a little crisp, about 5 minutes. Remove with a slotted spoon to a bowl. Increase the heat and add the beef, in 2 batches, breaking it up with a wooden spoon as it fries. Cook until well browned (about 5 minutes per batch). Set each batch aside with the pancetta when it's ready. Add the onion to the same pan with a pinch of salt, reduce the heat and cook until nice and soft, about 10 minutes. Add the garlic and cook for a further 30 seconds or so until smelling delicious.

2. Return the meats to the pan and pour in the passata, tomato purée, red wine and stock, give everything a stir and bring to a simmer. Leave to bubble away merrily for 1 hour, stirring every now and then, and topping up with water if necessary – you don't want the mixture to be too dry.

3. Reduce the heat and add the cream, pasta squares, Parmesan and mozzarella and stir it all together.

4. Meanwhile, cook your fries according to the packet instructions, either in the oven or (our favourite method) by frying them in plenty of hot oil. Pop them into a large skillet or serving dish.

5. Go wild – empty the whole lasagne sauce over the fries and sprinkle with extra Parmesan.

BBQ CHICKEN LOADED FRIES

1. Preheat the oven to 160°C/325°F/gas 3.

2. Place the chicken in a small roasting pan, pour over the barbecue sauce and cover with foil. Bake for 1 hour, flipping the chicken halfway through. Remove the chicken from the oven, shred with 2 forks and season to taste.

3. Increase the oven temperature to 200°C/400°F/gas 6. Meanwhile, cook your fries according to the packet instructions, either in the oven or by frying them in plenty of hot oil.

4. Pop the cooked fries into a large deep baking tray. Spoon the chicken on top and cover with the grated cheese. Chuck in the oven for 10 minutes.

5. Meanwhile, mix together the sauce ingredients and transfer to a squeezy bottle or piping bag (or bowl, to just dollop it on with a spoon).

6. When the cheese is all melted and nice, artfully top with your sauce, crispy bacon and jalapeños.

ROASTED GARLIC TARTIFLETTE SKINS

Often the best meals are the ones that transport you to somewhere else. Eating these, it's not hard to imagine yourself in front of a roaring fire in a wood cabin in the French Alps. There's a certain je ne sais quoi about an oozing Reblochon and salty bacon lardons that goes perfectly with crispy potato skins, giving you a creamy slice of comfort whether you like snow sports or just gorging on cream and cheese.

SERVES 6–8

7 banana shallots, peeled and quartered lengthways

2 whole garlic heads

100ml (generous ⅓ cup) water

2 tbsp white wine vinegar

1 tbsp caster (superfine) sugar

1 tsp olive oil

120g (4½oz) extra-thick streaky bacon lardons

3½ tbsp white wine

175ml (¾ cup) double (heavy) cream

1 x 240g (8½oz) Petit Reblochon cheese, cut into slices (a Camembert would be fine, if you can't find one)

salt and freshly ground black pepper, to taste

pickled cornichons and green salad, to serve

Skins:

4 large baking potatoes

olive oil, for drizzling

flaked sea salt, for sprinkling

1. Preheat the oven to 180°C/350°F/gas 4.

2. Pierce the skin of the potatoes and microwave them on high for roughly 15 minutes, or until a knife goes through them easily. Alternatively, bake them in an oven preheated to 200°C/400°F/gas mark 6 for 1 hour, or until easily pierced with a knife. Cut them in half and carefully scoop out the potato in the middle to make a boat shape, being careful not to break the skin. Set the mash aside for another worthy task (perhaps our Mashed Potato Dippers recipe on **p.221**).

3. Place the skins in a roasting pan, drizzle with olive oil and sprinkle with salt. Roast for 1 hour or so until really crispy.

4. Place the shallots in a separate roasting pan along with the garlic, pour in the water and add the vinegar and sugar (this will reduce and leave it all tasting delicious). Roast for 1 hour, or until the garlic is soft in its skin and the shallots have reduced to a jammy consistency. Give it a stir every now and then and top up with more water if necessary.

5. Heat the olive oil in a small saucepan over a medium heat and fry the bacon lardons for 3–4 minutes until they have taken on some colour but are not too crisp, then add the white wine to deglaze the pan. Turn down the heat to just a whisper, then pour in the cream and allow the mixture to reduce at barely a simmer for 5 minutes until thick. Squeeze the roasted garlic out of its skins into the cream mixture, then season to taste.

6. Carefully spoon the roasted shallots and creamy bacon sauce into the skins and top with a few decent slices of Reblochon per potato skin.

7. Put them back into the oven to bake until the cheese has melted. Serve hot with pickles and green salad.

LASAGNE DAUPHINOIS

Layers of creamy, cheesy beef ragu between perfectly cooked potatoes brings two of our all-time favourite dishes together. What follows is a labour of love; it took several goes to get it just perfect, but we cracked it eventually.

SERVES 6

1.1kg (2lb 7oz) small, equal-sized Maris Piper potatoes, peeled

1l (generous 4 cups) whole (full-fat) milk, plus extra if necessary

½ medium onion

2 bay leaves

50g (3½ tbsp) unsalted butter

40g (generous ¼ cup) plain (all-purpose) flour

80g (generous 1 cup) Parmesan, finely grated, plus extra for layering the lasagne

1 x recipe quantity Meat Ragu **(p.25)**

200g (7oz) pizza mozzarella or sliced mozzarella

salt and freshly ground black pepper, to taste

1. Preheat the oven to 160°C/325°F/gas 3.

2. Very thinly slice your potatoes (or, even better, use a mandoline) and place them in a wide, deep sauté pan, along with the milk, onion half and bay leaves. Season well with salt and pepper. Bring to a simmer and gently cook for about 7–10 minutes until the point of a knife goes through the potatoes easily (keep an eye on those on the bottom, as they tend to stick to the pan). Carefully remove to a plate with a slotted spoon. Discard the bay leaves and onion.

3. Pour the remaining milk into a measuring jug. If there's any less than 700ml (3 cups), pour in some fresh milk in to bring it up to quantity.

4. Heat the butter in a large saucepan over a medium heat until foaming, then add the flour and cook for 1–2 minutes until it smells biscuity. Gradually add the milk, beating all the time with a wooden spoon to remove any lumps, until you have a smooth béchamel sauce. Remove from the heat, beat in the Parmesan and season with salt and pepper to taste.

5. Grab yourself a large ovenproof cast-iron pan or lasagne dish and lightly grease with butter. Spoon in a thin layer of béchamel, then arrange a third of the cooked potatoes over the top, before topping with a third of the meat ragu and a third of the remaining béchamel sauce. Scatter over a third of the mozzarella and grate over some extra Parmesan. Repeat the layers – potatoes, ragu, béchamel, cheeses. Stop at the third layer, ensuring to use up all the remaining béchamel sauce.

6. Bake for 1 hour, or until the top is wonderfully golden. Bring out of the oven to sit for 15 minutes, then serve (with a salad, you animal).

CHEESY HASH BROWN

This one does what it says on the tin. Fried or poached eggs are great with this, as is the homemade ketchup on p.27.

SERVES 6

1.2kg (2lb 10oz) floury potatoes
(such as Maris Piper)

100g (½ cup) goose fat (or other fat of
your choosing), or extra as necessary

3 large onions, sliced into half-moons

150g (1½ cups) mature
Cheddar, grated

1 tbsp freshly ground black pepper

salt, to taste

Twisted Ketchup **(p.27)** and fried
eggs, to serve

1. Peel and grate the potatoes on a fine mandoline attachment, placing them to soak in a large bowl of cold water as you go. Rinse the potatoes very well to remove the starch, then leave to soak in a fresh batch of water for about 30 minutes.

2. Drain and dry the potatoes well, then (working in batches) spread them out on a wide plate and microwave on high for 4 minutes. Spread all of the par-cooked potatoes over a large baking tray and pop in the freezer to chill completely.

3. Place a non-stick sauté pan over a medium-high heat and add half of your goose fat. Chuck in the onions, season with salt and sauté for 20–30 minutes, stirring frequently, until lightly caramelised and translucent, but still holding their shape. Transfer to a bowl to cool completely.

4. Once the potatoes are cold, combine them with the cooled onions and grated cheese and season with the black pepper and 2 tsp salt. Mix well until everything is evenly distributed.

5. Heat the remaining fat in the same pan over a medium heat. Carefully spoon in the hash brown mixture and gently press down into an even layer. Cook for 10 minutes, shaking the pan occasionally, until crisp and golden underneath. Flip the cake out onto a plate, then slide it back into the pan (cooked-side up!), adding a little more fat if you think it needs it. Continuing cooking over a medium heat for a further 10 minutes, or until evenly crisp and golden.

6. Serve immediately with ketchup and fried eggs.

FRUIT

TREE OF
40 Fruit

TO ANYONE WHO THINKS THEY KNOW A BIT ABOUT BIOLOGY, THE IDEA OF A SINGLE TREE PRODUCING 40 DIFFERENT FRUIT SOUNDS SUSPICIOUSLY LIKE A SCIENCE EXPERIMENT GONE BADLY WRONG.

We've all seen enough low-budget sci-fi to know what can happen if you mess with Mother Nature. However, thanks to a pioneering New York-based artist, such a tree is no longer a nightmarish flight of fancy, but a living, breathing testament to what can be accomplished if you're prepared to push boundaries.

When he started his career, Sam Van Aken was much more interested in messing with public perception than he was with growing produce. Before he became the Frankenstein of fruit, he used to spend his time hijacking radio stations, playing fake adverts and songs to baffled audiences expecting to tune in to their favourite DJ.

It was this interest in creating the unexpected that eventually led Van Aken to the miracle of grafting. The technique, which has been a prominent feature of horticulture for thousands of years, allows tissues from different plants to bind and grow together on the same tree. From one trunk, it becomes possible to have individual branches bearing completely distinct species of fruit. Although this process is traditionally used to protect plants and increase the speed at which a crop can be produced, Van Aken was determined to explore grafting's limits.

After acquiring three acres of foreclosed orchard from the New York State Agricultural Experimental Station, he set about creating the first of his now internationally famous 'Trees of 40 Fruit'. Taking samples from each of the orchard's unique species, Van Aken grafted them all onto the main stem of one tree, creating a hybrid that can produce everything from nectarines, to peaches, to almonds, all at the same time.

Over the coming years, Van Aken created several other trees, each capable of yielding more than three-dozen different fruit species at once. He travelled all over the United States, planting everywhere from New York to Maine. Today, there are almost 20 separate sites. Every spring sees a lilac kaleidoscope of different flowers emerge from a single source, followed by fruit of every shape and size. Food and magic don't often mix; Van Aken and his trees might be the best way we have of bringing the two together.

The battle of the oranges

Food fights might fall out of favour as we get older, but there are a few occasions where it's still acceptable for anyone to pick up their dinner and use it as a weapon. Every year, in the small Italian town of Ivrea, locals gather to celebrate and recreate the ousting of a twelfth-century tyrant and his henchmen by dividing into nine separate squads and assaulting each other with around 500,000 pounds of freshly picked oranges.

The largest food fight in Italy, fought over three days, the Battle of the Oranges is so violent that participants are required to wear medieval-style suits of armour in order to stay safe. The onslaught often leaves townspeople covered in scars and bruises, before hostilities are brought to an abrupt end in preparation for a huge feast in the town square.

RENT A PINEAPPLE

Pineapples have fallen on hard times. Back in the eighteenth century, they graced the parties of the rich and famous up and down the country, basking in the glory of being weird-looking, exotic and really expensive. If you couldn't afford the £8,000 price tag to actually own one, you could rent and carry one around with you, a bit like a spiky Chanel bag – sexy! Sadly, they are no longer the aspirational fruit du jour (how the mighty have fallen, avocados), so spare a thought next time you pass that dusty inhabitant of your local greengrocer.

BAKED APPLE CRUMBLE CHEESECAKE

Apple crumble is the archetypal English pudding. It brings to mind a perfect country kitchen table, surrounded by hearty, pink-cheeked children, all clamouring around a steaming earthenware dish full of sweet apples and crunchy bits. We've channelled this general vibe of homely smugness into an easy baked cheesecake that is stunningly delicious and very easy to make.

SERVES 8

Apple filling:

5 peeled, cored and roughly chopped apples (preferably a type that keeps its shape when cooked, e.g. Granny Smith or Pink Lady)

100g (½ cup) soft light brown sugar

1 tsp ground cinnamon

Crumble:

80g (generous ⅓ cup) soft light brown sugar

80g (scant ⅔ cup) plain (all-purpose) flour

80g (⅓ cup) cold unsalted butter, cubed

40g (½ cup) rolled (old-fashioned) oats

Base:

12 digestive biscuits (Graham crackers)

60g (¼ cup) butter, melted, plus a little extra for greasing

a pinch of salt

Cheesecake mixture:

600g (2⅔ cups) cream cheese

250g (generous 1 cup) mascarpone

1 vanilla pod, seeds scraped

150g (¾ cup) caster (superfine) sugar

2 large eggs

5 tbsp plain (all-purpose) flour, sifted

60g (½ cup) icing (confectioners') sugar, sifted

1. Preheat the oven to 180°C/350°F/gas 4. Grease and line the base and sides of a 23cm (9in) springform cake pan (to make it easier to slide the cheesecake off the base later, flip it so the lip is facing downwards).

2. Mix the apples, sugar and cinnamon in a baking tray and bake for around 45 minutes, or until the apples have softened and the sugar has melted. Check halfway through and add a splash of water if anything looks like it's caramelising too quickly. Remove to cool and turn the oven down to 160°C/325°F/gas 3.

3. Put all of the crumble ingredients into a food processor and pulse until the mixture has come together into pea-sized pebbles. Tip out onto a tray, cover with clingfilm (plastic wrap)and set aside.

4. For the base, add the biscuits to the food processor and pulse until broken down. Add the melted butter and salt and continue to pulse until you have a damp, sand-like mixture.

5. Evenly press the biscuit base into the lined pan until compact.

6. For the cheesecake mix, using a hand-held whisk (or stand mixer), thoroughly combine cream cheese, mascarpone, vanilla seeds and sugar in a large bowl. Add the eggs, one by one, mixing between each addition. Thoroughly fold in the flour and finally the icing sugar. The resulting mixture shouldn't be too wet – balance an apple piece on top; if it sinks, fold in more icing sugar until the mixture is a bit stiffer.

7. Fill the cake pan with the cheesecake mixture, spreading it evenly over the biscuit base. Add all the baked apples in an even layer, then sprinkle over the crumble topping.

8. Bake for 1 hour 15 minutes. The cheesecake should have risen evenly, have a slight wobble and the crumble should be crunchy and golden.

9. Remove from the oven and allow to cool, then place in the refrigerator for at least 3 hours to set, before releasing from the pan.

GLAZED RASPBERRY CHEESECAKE ROLLS

Raspberries are definitely the queen of berries – sweet yet sharp, here they are resting on a sweet throne of soft dough, shrouded in the royal cloak of silky cheesecake. Warm from the oven and glazed with icing, these are absolutely stunning.

SERVES 12

Dough:

240ml (1 cup) milk, warmed

135g (⅔ cup) granulated sugar

1½ tbsp fast-action dried yeast (about 1½ sachets)

115g (½ cup) unsalted butter, softened to room temperature, plus extra for greasing

½ tsp fine sea salt

2 large eggs

565g (4¼ cups) plain (all-purpose) flour, plus extra for dusting

Filling:

225g (1 cup) cream cheese, softened

60g (¼ cup) unsalted butter, at room temperature

125g (scant ⅔ cup) caster (superfine) sugar

1 tsp vanilla extract

zest of 1 lemon

600g (1lb 5oz) frozen raspberries

2 tbsp cornflour (cornstarch)

Glaze:

125g (1 cup) icing (confectioners') sugar, sifted

60ml (¼ cup) double (heavy) cream

1. In a large bowl, combine the warm milk, sugar and yeast and let it sit for about 5 minutes until frothy.

2. Add the softened butter, salt, eggs and flour to the bowl and mix well until a dough forms. Place into a greased bowl, then cover and let rise in a warm place for about 1 hour or until the dough has doubled in size.

3. Meanwhile, preheat the oven to 200°C/400°F/gas 6. Grease and line a 23 x 33cm (9 x 13in) baking dish with baking paper.

4. In a large bowl, using a hand-held mixer or a wooden spoon, beat together the cream cheese, butter, sugar, vanilla and lemon zest until smooth.

5. Mix the frozen raspberries with the cornflour until well coated. Set aside.

6. Punch the dough down and roll it out on a lightly floured surface to a rectangle about 46 x 30cm (18 x 12in) and about 5mm (¼in) thick.

7. Spread the cream cheese mixture evenly over the dough, then spread over the frozen raspberries. Tightly roll the dough into a long log, then cut into 12 equal rolls. Arrange the rolls, with the swirls facing up, in the prepared baking dish. Cover and let rise for about 30 minutes.

8. Bake for 25–35 minutes until golden brown and bubbly. Remove and let cool a little.

9. Mix together icing sugar and cream for the glaze until smooth, then top the rolls while they are still warm. Enjoy!

CINNAMON-SWIRL APPLE PIE

This was the most viral video we've ever had, clocking up an obscene 137 million views (and counting) since Christmas Day 2017. That's slightly less than the population of Russia. This almost incomprehensibly large horde of Twisted fans obviously knew we were on to something – swirls are fun.

SERVES 8

60g (¼ cup) unsalted butter, melted

4 x sheets ready-made shortcrust pastry, chilled

800g (8 cups) tart apples (such as Granny Smiths), peeled, cored and thinly sliced

150g (¾ cup) golden caster (superfine) sugar

1 tsp ground cinnamon

3 tbsp plain (all-purpose) flour

1 egg, beaten with a little milk

Vanilla ice cream, to serve (optional)

Cinnamon sprinkle:

1 tbsp ground cinnamon

1 tbsp caster (superfine) sugar

1. Preheat the oven to 180°C/350°F/gas 4. Grease a 23cm (9in) pie dish with butter.

2. Mix together the cinnamon sprinkle ingredients.

3. Unroll or roll out 1 pastry sheet, brush it all over with the melted butter and sprinkle evenly with some of the cinnamon sprinkle mixture. Tightly roll the pastry into a log and cut it along its length into 5mm (¼in) wide rounds. Repeat with the remaining pastry sheets.

4. Arrange half of the rounds next to each other in the pie dish. Press down firmly so that they form a swirly crust with no gaps, right to the edges of the dish. Brush with egg wash and set aside.

5. Toss the apples with the sugar, cinnamon and flour until well coated, then tip the mixture into the prepared crust.

6. Place a large sheet of greaseproof paper on your work surface and arrange the remaining pastry swirls on top in a circle, then top with another large sheet of greaseproof paper. Use a rolling pin to roll the pastry out between the sheets to about 5mm (¼in) thick. Remove one of the greaseproof sheets and use the other piece to help you place the pastry on top of the pie. Press down the edges to seal and trim off any excess pie crust with a sharp knife. Brush the top evenly with the remaining egg wash and cut a small cross in the top of the pie to let the steam escape.

7. Bake for 45 minutes until the apples are cooked through and the crust is golden brown.

8. Serve with vanilla ice cream. Enjoy!

UPSIDE-DOWN BANANA CAKE

Upside-down cakes are about as 70s as avocado bathrooms, cheese impaled on cocktail sticks and hirsute men in tight trousers. We've decided to revisit this simple but also deeply satisfying concept of fruit on top of cake, opting for the flavours of caramel, chocolate and banana in a richly satisfying pudding, best eaten warm.

SERVES 8

Topping:

50g (3½ tbsp) unsalted butter

80g (generous ⅓ cup) soft light brown sugar

80ml (⅓ cup) maple syrup

½ tsp cornflour (cornstarch), mixed with 1 tsp water

4 firm bananas (better for slicing)

Batter:

200g (generous ¾ cup) unsalted butter, softened

200g (1 cup) soft light brown sugar

3 medium eggs

100ml (generous ⅓ cup) whole (full-fat) milk

300g (2¼ cups) plain (all-purpose) flour

3 tsp baking powder

a pinch of salt

2 ripe bananas, mashed

100g (¾ cup) milk chocolate, evenly chopped

1. Preheat the oven to 180°C/350°F/gas 4. Line a 20cm (8in) square cake pan with baking paper.

2. Combine the butter, brown sugar and maple syrup in a saucepan set over a low heat. Cook, stirring frequently, until the sugar dissolves – don't allow it to boil over! Stir in the cornflour mixture to stabilise and thicken the caramel, then take it off the heat. Pour carefully into the cake pan.

3. Slice the bananas lengthways into about 4 pieces. Trim the ends to make squared-off slices, exactly 10cm (4in) in length. Place them snugly into the caramel in the pan in a single layer. Chill in the refrigerator for 30 minutes.

4. Meanwhile for the batter, put the butter and sugar into a large bowl and beat with an electric mixer until the mixture has lightened in colour. Add the eggs, one at a time, beating after each addition. Pour in the milk, then sift in the flour, baking powder and salt and fold in. Finally, fold in the mashed bananas and chocolate chips. Gently spoon the mixture over the sliced bananas and caramel, being careful not to move things around too much.

5. Place the cake pan on a baking tray (otherwise the caramel can leak out of the pan and make a mess) and bake for about 50 minutes until golden on top and an inserted skewer comes out clean.

6. Leave to cool in the pan for around 5 minutes, then turn out onto a serving plate. Be careful not to forget about it or it'll stick to the pan.

ETON MESS ICE CREAM SANDWICHES

Nothing screams summer like Eton Mess. Even normal members of society (those without straw boaters and an archaic sense of inherited privilege) recognise this as one of the most quintessentially English of desserts; it's basically cricket and the pub in pudding form. Our version takes this essence, turns it into an insanely tasty ice cream and thwacks it between two easy-to-handle pieces of slightly chewy meringue – gosh!

SERVES 9

Ice cream:

400g (14oz) ripe strawberries, quartered

3½ tbsp water

1 tsp lemon juice

3½ tbsp caster (superfine) sugar

1 tbsp vodka

600ml (2½ cups) double (heavy) cream

1 x 400ml (14fl oz) can sweetened condensed milk

Meringue:

5 large egg whites

220g (generous 1 cup) white caster (superfine) sugar

1 tsp white wine vinegar

1 tsp cornflour (cornstarch)

1. Combine the strawberries, water, lemon juice and sugar in a saucepan set over a low-medium heat and bring to a simmer. Cook until the strawberries have broken up and the liquid has become thick and jammy – this may take a while, but persevere as it's crucial to the setting of the no-churn ice cream that there is very little water in the mixture. Remove from the heat and let cool, then add the vodka (the alcohol will prevent the mixture from fully freezing). Set aside to cool completely.

2. Meanwhile, preheat the oven to 110°C/225°F/gas ¼ and line two 20cm (8in) square spingform cake pans with baking paper.

3. Whip the cream until it forms stiff peaks, then gently fold in the condensed milk. Pour into one of the cake pans and spoon the strawberry mixture on top, mixing it in with the point of a knife to make swirls. Transfer to the freezer until set, then remove from the cake pan. Place the block of ice cream on a tray or large plate and return to the freezer. Re-line the cake pan with another piece of baking paper.

4. Using a spotlessly clean mixing bowl and electric beaters, whisk the egg whites until they form soft peaks. Add the sugar, 1 tbsp at a time, whisking well between each addition, until the meringue is thick, glossy and will hold up in stiff, rope-like peaks on the end of the beaters. Add the vinegar and cornflour and whisk again until combined.

5. Using a large spoon, evenly divide the meringue between the 2 lined cake pans. Don't worry if the layer looks quite thin, they do rise during cooking. Bake for 2½ hours, then leave to cool.

6. When cool, remove the ice cream from the freezer. Remove the baking paper from the meringues and very gently turn one of them upside down. Place the block of ice cream on top, then place the other meringue on top to form a sandwich.

7. You're done! Leave them to sit out briefly before cutting into 9 squares. Dig in!

BLUEBERRY CHARLOTTE ROYALE

If you turn up at your local cake sale clutching this absolute beauty you'll be the envy of everyone, from children peddling sad cupcakes to mums bitterly clutching Victoria sponges. Don't worry though, despite being very impressive, it's deceptively easy to make. It does look a bit like a brain though.

SERVES 8

unsalted butter, for greasing

8 large eggs, separated

1 heaped tsp vanilla extract

230g (generous 1 cup) granulated sugar, plus 2½ tbsp

150g (generous 1 cup) plain (all-purpose) flour

125g (½ cup) blueberry jam (jelly)

Cheesecake filling:

500ml (generous 2 cups) double (heavy) cream

450g (2 cups) cream cheese, softened

125g (generous 1 cup) icing (confectioners') sugar, sifted

¾ tsp vanilla extract

1. Preheat the oven to 180°C/350°F/gas 4. Grease and line two 25 x 38cm (10 x 15in) deep baking trays with baking paper coming up the sides.

2. Place the egg yolks, vanilla and granulated sugar in a large bowl and whip with a hand-held electric mixer until the yolks have doubled in volume.

3. In a separate bowl, whip the egg whites on a medium speed until foamy, then gradually pour in the extra 2½ tbsp sugar and increase the speed to high, whipping until the whites hold a medium peak.

4. Sift the flour into the yolk mixture and fold in using a whisk, then fold in the whipped egg whites. Split the batter between the prepared pans, spreading it evenly.

5. Bake for 12 minutes until just springy to the touch. Let the sponges cool for about 2 minutes.

6. Spread the jam evenly over the sponges, then roll them up from the short side using the baking paper to help. Let cool completely.

7. Meanwhile, make the cheesecake filling. Whip the double cream to stiff peaks. In a separate bowl, beat the cream cheese, icing sugar and vanilla until smooth, then fold in the whipped cream until combined.

8. Line a large domed glass bowl with clingfilm (plastic wrap). Slice the sponge rolls into 1cm (½in) slices and use them to line the bowl, pressing them slightly together. Pour in the cheesecake mixture and spread evenly, then cover with the remaining sponge swirls. Cover with clingfilm and refrigerate for 4 hours or overnight.

9. Invert onto a serving plate and peel away the clingfilm. Slice and serve.

CHOCOLATE

MONTEZUMA'S
Chocolate Libido

MONTEZUMA II WAS A MAN OF MANY ODD APPETITES. AS THE EMPEROR OF THE ALL-POWERFUL AZTEC EMPIRE, HE OVERSAW ONE OF THE MOST INFAMOUS PERIODS IN CENTRAL AMERICAN HISTORY.

On a typical day, his royal duties could range from enthusiastically cheering on a human sacrifice, to bullying helpless Mesoamerican tribespeople. At the epicentre of this morally reprehensible routine was chocolate.

For the Aztecs, chocolate was much more than a last-minute gift idea for salvaging forgotten anniversaries. It was considered essential to many ritual aspects of everyday life and, as a result, was given the utmost respect. Rather than being bought and sold in sickly sweet bars, Aztec chocolate was always drunk as a rich, bitter liquid, served hot and mixed with water and local spices. For a time, frothy cups of cocoa sold from street stalls were a regular sight in both Aztec and earlier Mayan society.

By the time Montezuma came to power, cocoa was taken more seriously than ever. No longer was it something to be casually consumed in the street – chocolate was treated with complete reverence and held to be 'the food of the Gods'. As such, only certain people were allowed to enjoy it. Warriors were presented with steaming cups before heading into battle and nobles drank it as a post-dinner digestif. But perhaps its most interesting application was as a royal love drug.

In order that he might avoid an embarrassing instance of stage fright, Montezuma had his court come up with the world's original stiff drink. A mixture of liquid chocolate, honey and chilli pepper was poured into a golden goblet, before being ceremoniously presented to the God-King. Montezuma would then drink, walk out onto the palace balcony, hurl the empty cup over the edge into a nearby lake and prepare for action. This was, by all accounts, a daily ritual.

So successful was his courtiers' concoction, that Montezuma soon insisted on drinking nothing else. It was said that the chocoholic monarch could consume as many as 50 flagons every single day – that's equivalent to about 25 modern bar pitchers! Although there are serious questions over whether this habit made the slightest bit of difference in the bedroom, the randy ruler clearly felt it was paying off. Given this unsavoury context, a gift of chocolates for Valentine's Day no longer seems quite so sweet.

Bean counters

Cocoa was once used by the Mayans and Aztecs as a form of currency. In this fabulous bean's native country, ten cocoa pods could land you with a new pet rabbit, a new chair set for the garden perhaps! Even after the Spanish arrived in 1519, the beans were still used as an official form of currency.

It was noted by an early western observer of Aztec culture that cocoa beans 'yieldeth sweete and profitable drinke for mankinde, and preserveth the possessors thereof free from the hellish pestilence of avarice because it cannot be long kept hid underground'. An interesting concept – if money could 'go off' humanity would stop hoarding and burying it in weird places (here's looking at you, offshore banking!).

CHOCOLATE BOMB

When the tide of fortune turned against the Nazis in WWII, they clutched at some fairly ridiculous straws in an attempt to avoid defeat. One of the silliest was a cunning plan to assassinate the figurehead of the resistance, the famous cigar-chomper Winston Churchill. The plan was to smuggle a bomb disguised as choccy bar into Churchill's inner sanctum, where the sweet slab of death would explode, killing him and clearing the road for the Third Reich. Needless to say, it didn't come off.

TRIPLE CHOCOLATE MOCHA MOUSSE CAKE

A glorious celebration of everyone's two favourite beans – cocoa and coffee. Often, chocolate mousse involves raw egg whites (which can make certain people nervous in this age of food hygiene certificates), but ours simply uses whipped cream with chocolate folded into it. The resulting concoction is beautifully light and rich with the slight complexity of coffee.

SERVES 8–10

Base:

225g (8oz) digestive biscuits (32 squares Graham crackers)

85g (3oz) dark chocolate, broken into pieces

85g (6 tbsp) unsalted butter, melted and cooled

Mousse:

180ml (¾ cup) double (heavy) cream, at room temperature

2½ tsp instant coffee granules

200g (7oz) dark (plain unsweetened) chocolate, finely chopped

500ml (generous 2 cups) double or whipping (heavy) cream, chilled

4 tbsp icing (confectioners') sugar

1 heaped tsp vanilla extract

Ganache:

250ml (generous 1 cup) double (heavy) cream

225g (8oz) dark (plain unsweetened) chocolate, finely chopped

1. Grease and line the base of a 23cm (9in) springform cake pan with baking paper.

2. In a food processor, pulse the biscuits (crackers) until ground, then add the chocolate and pulse until the chocolate is in small chunks. Pour in the cooled butter and pulse to combine until the mixture is almost like wet sand. Pour the mixture into the lined cake pan and press down evenly (use the bottom of a measuring cup to help). Refrigerate for 30 minutes, or until needed.

3. Meanwhile, make the mousse filling. Add the room temperature cream and coffee to a microwavable jug. Heat in 30-second intervals until steaming but not boiling. Place the chopped chocolate into a bowl and pour over the hot cream, stirring until completely melted. Set aside to cool completely.

4. In a large bowl, whisk together the cold cream, icing sugar and vanilla until stiff peaks form. Be sure not to over-whip or it will become grainy and split.

5. Fold the cooled chocolate mixture into the whipped cream until just combined. Do this by gently folding from the bottom of the bowl over to the top – this will ensure all the whipped cream and chocolate are well incorporated. Spoon on top of the chilled biscuit base and use an offset spatula to evenly smooth the top. Chill for 4–6 hours to set (or overnight for best results).

6. Before serving, make the ganache topping. Heat the cream in the microwave (or on the hob) until steaming but not boiling, then pour it over the finely chopped chocolate. Let sit for 30 seconds, then stir to incorporate until smooth. Let cool slightly to thicken a bit.

7. Remove the set cake from the springform pan. Place it over a cooling rack set on top of a baking tray to catch the drips and evenly pour the chocolate ganache over the top. Gently tap the cooling rack on the counter a couple of times to help the chocolate spread. Return to the refrigerator and chill for 30 minutes, then serve.

CHEAT'S CHURROS & CHOCOLATE SAUCE

Most churro recipes involve the deeply irksome process of making choux pastry; whacking eggs into a greasy ball of dough, forcing it into piping bags, and cursing as you attempt to squeeze the resulting truculent mass through the nozzle – it's not pretty. Our recipe (which is probably secretly what most churro makers actually use) is a walk in the park in comparison, leaving you more time to do the more fun things in life (like eating churros).

SERVES 4

50g (3½ tbsp) unsalted butter

200ml (generous ¾ cup) hot water

150ml (⅔ cup) milk

100g (½ cup) granulated sugar

250g (scant 2 cups) plain (all-purpose) flour

1 tsp baking powder

neutral oil, for frying

2 tsp ground cinnamon

Chocolate sauce:

100ml (generous ⅓ cup) double (heavy) cream

150g (5½oz) dark (plain unsweetened) chocolate, finely chopped

1½ tbsp golden syrup

1. Put the butter, water and milk into a jug, along with 4 tsp of the sugar. Microwave for about 2 minutes until really hot. In a large bowl, whisk together the flour and baking powder, then pour the hot liquid into the flour mix and stir until a thick and smooth dough is formed. Let cool slightly.

2. Meanwhile, heat the oil in a deep, heavy saucepan to 175°C (350°F).

3. In a large bowl, mix together the remaining sugar with the cinnamon and set aside.

4. Transfer the dough mixture to a piping bag fitted with a large star nozzle. Carefully pipe strips of about 15cm (6in) long strips into the hot oil, snipping them off with kitchen scissors. Fry for 2–3 minutes until golden brown, then remove with a slotted spoon to drain briefly on kitchen paper.

5. While the churros are still warm, toss them in the cinnamon sugar to coat.

6. Meanwhile, make the sauce. Put the cream, chocolate and golden syrup into a microwavable jug and heat for 1 minute until the chocolate is melted. Stir to combine.

7. Serve the churros warm, with the chocolate sauce for dipping, or drizzled over the top.

BAILEYS ICE CUBE TRUFFLES

These ravishing truffles feature our favourite flavour combination: Baileys Irish Cream and chocolate. You can fill them with whatever you wish, but we think raspberries or hazelnuts are the perfect match. This is also, potentially, the most innovative use for an ice-cube tray we've ever seen.

SERVES 6

Ganache:

400g (14oz) dark (plain unsweetened) chocolate, finely chopped

100ml (generous ⅓ cup) double (heavy) cream

100ml (generous ⅓ cup) Baileys Irish Cream

Coating:

375g (13oz) dark (plain unsweetened) chocolate, finely chopped

1 tbsp coconut oil

White chocolate and raspberry truffles:

white chocolate, melted

fresh raspberries

Chocolate hazelnut truffles:

milk chocolate, melted

toasted hazelnuts

1. For white chocolate and raspberry truffles: drizzle melted white chocolate across an ice-cube tray, being sure to get it on all the sides. Chill in the refrigerator for 10 minutes.

2. For chocolate hazelnut truffles: repeat the above step with a melted milk chocolate drizzle. Next, make the coating: put the chocolate and coconut oil into a microwavable jug and microwave on high in 30-second increments until completely melted. Pour the coating into the ice-cube trays and tilt the trays in all directions, allowing the chocolate to cover the sides. Flip the trays upside-down to let any excess chocolate drip out (reserve the excess), then refrigerate for 5 minutes.

3. To make the ganache, put the chocolate in a large bowl. Put the cream and Baileys into a microwavable jug and microwave until steaming, then pour over the chocolate and let sit for 1 minute. Stir to combine until smooth.

4. Fill each ice-cube tray indentation one-third full of ganache.

5. For white chocolate and raspberry truffles: Add a raspberry to each white chocolate truffle, then cover it with ganache and smooth over. Top each indentation up with the chocolate coating mixture and smooth over.

6. For chocolate hazelnut truffles: Repeat the above step for the milk chocolate tray, with a hazelnut in each indentation.

7. For plain truffles: Fill the indentations of an ice-cube tray two-thirds full with ganache and seal with the chocolate coating mixture.

8. Chill all trays for 15–20 minutes until set. Carefully pop the truffles out and trim off excess chocolate if needed. Wrap 'em up if you're planning on giving them to someone as a present, or just treat yourself!

TOASTED HAZELNUT BROWNIES

What makes a perfect brownie is something that can spark fierce debate. Wars have been fought over less. At the end of the day, like most things, it's subjective.* Do you consider nuts an utter abomination? Do you even like brownies? Is it possible to find meaning or certainty in a world in constant flux?

*This brownie recipe is definitely, without a doubt, the best you'll ever make – if you don't think so, you're wrong.

SERVES 6

300g (1⅓ cups) unsalted butter

300g (10½oz) chocolate (85% cocoa solids), broken into pieces

4 large eggs

300g (1½ cups) caster (superfine) sugar

100g (½ cup) soft light brown sugar

a pinch of flaked sea salt, plus extra for sprinkling

120g (scant 1 cup) self-raising flour

80g (scant ⅔ cup) plain (all-purpose) flour

50g (½ cup) unsweetened cocoa powder

120g (scant 1 cup) toasted hazelnuts

1. Preheat the oven to 180°C/350°F/gas 4. Grease and line a 23cm (9in) square cake pan with baking paper.

2. Place the butter in a Pyrex jug and heat in the microwave (or on the hob) in 30-second bursts until piping hot.

3. Place the chocolate pieces in a bowl and pour over the hot melted butter, stirring until the mixture is completely smooth. Set aside to cool.

4. In a large bowl, whisk together the eggs and sugars until the mixture is thoroughly combined, smooth and light.

5. Add the (cooled) chocolate mixture to the eggs and sugar and stir to make a glossy batter. Add a small pinch of salt, then sift in the flours and cocoa powder and gently fold through to incorporate. Finally, stir in the toasted nuts.

6. Pour the batter into the lined cake pan. Bake for 20 minutes, or until the edges look cooked but the middle still has a slight wobble.

7. We like to leave our brownies to set completely in the refrigerator as they become deliciously thick and fudgy, but you can also eat them immediately, sprinkled with a little sea salt, if you wish.

A NICE CHOCOLATE CAKE

This has it all – it's light yet rich and decadently chocolatey. Three layers make it an imposingly delicious celebration cake.

SERVES 8–10

375g (generous 2¾ cups)
plain (all-purpose) flour

675g (3⅓ cups) granulated sugar

110g (generous 1 cup)
unsweetened cocoa powder

1 tbsp baking powder

2¼ tsp bicarbonate of soda
(baking soda)

1 tsp salt

2 tsp instant coffee granules

375ml (generous 1½ cups) milk

185ml (¾ cup) vegetable oil

3 large eggs, whisked

3 tsp vanilla extract

350ml (1½ cups) boiling water

chocolate shavings, to decorate

Ganache:

200g (7oz) dark (plain unsweetened)
chocolate, chopped

450g (1lb) milk chocolate, chopped

675ml (generous 2¾ cups) double
(heavy) cream

1. Preheat the oven to 180°C/350°F/gas 4. Grease and line the base of 3 x 20cm (8in) cake pans with baking paper.

2. In a large bowl or a stand mixer, combine the flour, sugar, cocoa, baking powder, bicarbonate of soda, salt and instant coffee. Whisk through or use the paddle attachment to stir through the mixture until well combined.

3. Add the milk, vegetable oil, eggs and vanilla and mix together on a medium speed until well combined. Reduce the speed and carefully add the boiling water to the batter until well combined.

4. Distribute the batter evenly between the 3 cake pans and bake for 30–35 minutes until an inserted toothpick or skewer comes out clean.

5. Remove from the oven and allow to cool in the cake pans for about 10 minutes, then remove the sponges from the pans to a wire rack to cool completely.

6. Put the chopped chocolates for the ganache into a large bowl. In a microwavable jug (or on the hob), heat the cream for 2 minutes until steaming, then pour over the chocolate. Let sit for 5 minutes, then stir to incorporate. Set aside at room temperature until thickened.

7. Place a layer of sponge on your serving plate and top with ganache. Top this with another layer of sponge and repeat. When the third layer is placed, cover the entire cake with the remaining ganache. Shave chocolate all over the top of the cake to decorate.

8. Slice and enjoy!

COOKIES & CREAM ZEBRA ROLL

There are very few occasions in life when cheating is fine, but this is one of them, and it makes your job a lot easier. Cake mix from a box is perfect for this recipe, creating a light and flexible sponge that copes particularly well with being rolled up.

SERVES 6

6 large eggs

70ml (⅓ cup) sour cream

3½ tbsp water

3½ tbsp vegetable oil

1 x 425g (15oz) packet vanilla cake mix

50g (½ cup) unsweetened cocoa powder

Filling:

190g (generous ¾ cup) cream cheese

150ml (⅔ cup) double or whipping (heavy) cream

4½ tbsp icing (confectioners') sugar

75g (¾ cup) crushed chocolate sandwich cookies

1. Preheat the oven to 180°C/350°F/gas 4. Line a 25 x 38cm (10 x 15in) deep baking tray with baking paper.

2. Beat the eggs in a large bowl until light in colour and frothy, about 5 minutes. Add the sour cream, water, oil and cake mix, then use an electric mixer on low speed to mix until combined. Gently stir with a spatula.

3. Split the batter in half and add the cocoa to one half, whisking to combine. Place the vanilla and chocolate batters in individual piping bags with small holes cut at the tip.

4. Pipe alternating lines of vanilla and chocolate batter diagonally across the tray. Use any leftover batter for making some fun cupcakes!

5. Tap the tray on the counter about 3 times to pop any air bubbles. Bake for 7–8 minutes until the cake is spongy and springs back slightly when touched.

6. While it is still hot, carefully flip the sponge onto a clean tea (dish) towel. Let cool slightly, then use the towel to help you roll up the sponge from the long edge, tightly but carefully. Set aside to cool for 30–40 minutes.

7. Meanwhile, make the filling. Whip together the cream cheese, cream and icing sugar until stiff peaks form.

8. Gently unroll the cooled sponge and evenly spread over the cream cheese mixture, leaving about 1cm (½in) clear at the end. Sprinkle the crushed cookies over the top, then evenly and tightly roll the sponge back up.

9. Chill in the refrigerator for 15 minutes until set, then slice into rounds and serve.

INDEX

D

ACKNOWLEDGEMENTS

To the entire Twisted team, past and present: Hugh, Tara, Thomas, Alice, Marcus, Alex, Sophie, Jordan, Charly, Nathan, Tassy and Hayden. To the entire Jungle Creations family for making Twisted what it is today, and for making this book possible. To Jamie for the opportunity, the vision, the lot. To Mel for letting us crack on with it, and generally just being legit. To all of our amazing contributors to this book — all of your unique and personal contributions encapsulate our vision of Twisted as a true collective; to Louise, Alex and Valerie for your incredible creativity; to David and Rosie for your effortless eye and sense of fun; to our illustrators, Rose, Jessie and Henri, for your immense talent (and fortitude when faced with the brief). To Chris, Tom and the team at LoveGunn — what a mission! To Emily for your appreciation for detail and unfathomable patience (and for making us sound good). To Lydia and Rose and all of our significant others for putting up with us.

Finally, to you. If you have ever watched one of our videos, bought some loaded fries from one of our restaurants, popped into our pop-up bar, cooked something a bit weird with your loved ones and laughed about it, stepped out of your comfort zone and tried something new — any or all of the above — thank you. This book is (literally) yours.

First published in Great Britain in 2020 by Hodder & Stoughton
An Hachette UK Company

1

Text copyright © Jungle Creations Limited 2020
hi@twisted.team
Occasions Photography © Louise Hagger 2019
Ingredients Photography © David Loftus 2019
Lifestyle Photography by Kenzo Ejiri 2019

A CIP catalogue record for this title is available from the British Library

Hardback ISBN: 978 1 529 39484 9
Ebook ISBN: 978 1 529 39483 2

Colour Origination by Altaimage

Printed and bound by Firmengruppe APPL, aprinta druck, Wemding, Germany

Hodder & Stoughton's policy is to use papers that are neutral, renewable and recyclable products and made from wood grown in sustainable forests. The logging and manufacturing processes are expected to conform to the environmental regulations of the country of origin.

DESIGN
LoveGunn

TEXT
Tom Jackson (Introduction, Recipes and Stories); Tara Maini (Recipes);
Hugh Woodward (Recipes and Stories); Thomas Lethbridge (Stories); Alex Duncan (Drinks)

PHOTOGRAPHY
David Loftus (Ingredients); Louise Hagger (Occasions); Kenzo Ejiri (Lifestyle)
Laura Heckford (Assistant, Occasions)

FOOD STYLING
Rosie Scott (Ingredients); Valerie Berry (Occasions)

PROP STYLING
Alexander Breeze (Occasions)

ILLUSTRATION
Henri Campeã (Ingredients); Jessie Kanelos Weiner (Stories);
Rose Electra Harris (Basics)

CREATIVE DIRECTION
Tom Jackson

COPY-EDITOR
Emily Preece-Morrison

FOOD EDITOR
Tom Jackson

SPECIAL CONTRIBUTION
Harry Bamber